NO MERCY?

The True Story of One Man's Thirst for Revenge

by

BRIAN RUSS

INSPIRATION PUBLICATIONS

Published in Great Britain by
Inspiration Publications
PO Box 568, Devizes, Wiltshire SN10 1QL

Copyright © Brian Russ 1996

First published in 1996 by Inspiration Publications

ISBN 0 9526712 0 4

Printed in Great Britain by
Redwood Books, Trowbridge, Wiltshire.
Typeset by Avonset, Midsomer Norton, Bath.
Cover designed by Create Publishing, Bath.

CONTENTS

ACKNOWLEDGEMENTS

With deep gratitude to my wife Judith
and daughter Leoni for their support.
Also to my friend Nelly Thomas.

A special thanks to Brian Kellock and
many others for the help they gave me.

Chapter One

CONDEMNED

On arriving home I poured myself a drink, and gathered up the remainder of my pills. With a two fingered gesture to the world, I swallowed the lethal mixture and got into bed. I took great comfort in the knowledge that I wouldn't wake up again. There was no fear or concern about death, just relief to be free of pain. I had taken enough drugs to kill myself three times, so I was confident my life was over.

The pillow felt soft as my head rested against it. For the first time in my life I'd achieved something which no one could take from me. With heavy eyes and a blank mind, I lost consciousness.

The first thing I became aware of, was how relaxed I felt, and if this was death it was great. However as I opened my eyes, I was horrified to find out that I was still in my flat and very much alive.

'No! I can't be alive,' I shouted angrily,'I don't want to be.'

The reality of another day struggling through life depressed me. 'What have you got to do to get out of this world?' I said angrily. I started to head butt the wall, as I blamed myself for the failure. 'You can't even do that right, you idiot.'

After a while I stopped punishing myself, and began pacing the floor. It was a mystery to me, why I wasn't dead, or at least feeling ill. I should have been sick or hung-over, but I was fine. I sat in the chair and opened a bottle of booze, and started to recall how I ended up this mess.

My mind went back four years to 1982, when I lived in the flat with a girlfriend. We were engaged and had planned to marry within two years. We had been living together for three years and we both thought we'd be together always. Our relationship hadn't been without it's troubles and opposition but we always got through it.

I had been working for some time on a construction site, and had just established my own building contracts. Suddenly without any warning I was taken ill, and admitted to hospital with chest pains. I was discharged the next day when I was told all I needed was a short rest. Over the next month I experienced frightening attacks of choking and breathlessness.

All this came as quite a shock to me. I'd hardly ever had a day's illness in my life, and certainly never been in hospital. The doctors didn't seem interested as they kept saying there wasn't anything wrong with me.

I was reduced from a powerfully built fourteen stone man, to a weak bag of bones. My face was ashen and gaunt and my eyes were set back in their sockets. My imagination had run riot thinking all kinds of dreadful thoughts including the possibility of cancer. After three months of torment and a loss of four stone in weight, I was finally told what was wrong.

'You're suffering from chronic anxiety,' said my doctor smiling. 'Now go home and don't worry anymore.'

'Not worry!' I thought, 'I've got chronic anxiety and he tells me not to worry. I don't know what chronic anxiety is, but it sounds pretty serious to me.'

'Can you tell me what anxiety is?' I asked.

'Just go home and relax, have a glass of beer,' he said.

'Will the symptoms go away?' I asked, hopefully.

'I'll put you on a course of pills, they're new, and will soon sort you out. Goodbye, and send in the next person please.'

I left feeling more confused than ever, but hoped the pills he gave me would clear it up. Sadly things got worse, as I started to suffer with the shakes. As I walked back into the doctors surgery, I could see he wasn't pleased to see me.

'What is it this time?' he asked, sounding exasperated.

I sat down, my hands were trembling. 'Please help me my whole body is going out of control,' I cried.

'I'm feeling a bit that way myself,' he said sharply. 'I'm afraid you've got to face it; you're a worrier like the rest of your family.'

'Is it the pills?' I asked.

'I should say it's more likely to be you,' he said, sternly. 'You've got to pull yourself together, now take these anti-depressants instead, but give them time to work.'

I felt ashamed and pathetic as I left the surgery. In the morning I woke to find my balance had gone, making it difficult to stand up. 'I must try to relax I thought,' so I ran a hot bath. I had hardly been in the bath five minutes, when my heart started pounding faster and faster. It got so fast it felt as if it was about to explode. I leapt out of the bath as I started to panic. Without bothering to get dry, I quickly put on my trousers. I thought I must be cracking up so I threw a glass at the door in an attempt to snap myself out of it, but it didn't break. As the seconds passed there was no sign of my heart rate slowing and now I was beginning to struggle for breath.

Convinced that I was having a heart attack, I opened my flat door and dashed outside onto the landing. I shouted for help, but there was no help to be had. I felt so alone. There had never been anyone around, the times I needed someone. I grew up alone and now I was going to die alone.

'That's it then, is it? I'll just die right here!' I shouted angrily. But there was nobody listening, all the doors in the block of flats remained closed. With an unwillingness to give in, I tried to get to hospital myself.

By the time I reached the hospital entrance, I was almost off my head. I was taken to a side ward where they just told me to lay still. They briefly checked me over and sent me on my way.

'You can't mean me to go home surely,' I pleaded.

'It's only anxiety,' said a nurse, 'and I don't know what a young man like you has got to worry about.'

'I'm only worried, because I don't know what's happening to me,' I said.

My heart rate had become too fast to keep count, and my blood pressure felt sky high, but they didn't seem interested. Reluctantly I left, only to return twice more that day with the same problem. My girlfriend wasn't happy about my frequent disappearances, but I couldn't help it.

'Another day like this one, will certainly finish me off,' I thought.

Morning came and fortunately I had an appointment at the surgery made for me by the hospital. I hardly dared to look the doctor in the face as I entered his room.

'I should think that nice girl will probably leave you. She's far too good for you. Here is a prescription for valium, take thirty miiligrams a day and stop taking all the other pills. Now stop pestering the surgery, because there are lots of other patients,' he said.

All the time I was in there I was never asked how I was or even given the chance to speak. I sat outside the surgery for a while, as I was too frightened to move. Eventually my co-ordination returned and I started to feel better.

Some time later I heard how the first drug I'd been given had been taken off the market. Apparently it caused too many side effects which affected the nervous system. It was that, which had pushed my adrenalin levels too high, causing my heart to go out of control. It had overloaded my nervous system so much that I lost my balance.

My health slowly started to get better as the valium began to take effect in my system. After three months of an involuntary diet, I was once again able to eat and swallow food. Just when I was regaining my confidence, I was stricken with pneumonia.

All the weight I had managed to put back on fell away in a couple of nights. I found myself in and out of hospital with recurring health problems.

The family of my fiancee came to see me. 'We feel that you have a weak character, not that it's your fault,' they said. 'However you're going to have to pull yourself together for our daughter's sake.' I didnt reply, but inside I felt bitter. 'What do they think I have been doing?' I thought. Nobody was prepared to help, but they were all pretty quick to pass judgement.

My confidence was completely wiped out and I found the most simple of tasks virtually impossible. I had become so obsessed with myself and how I was feeling, that I hardly knew anyone else was there, let alone consider their feelings. I just didn't have time for anyone else, as it took all my energy just to stay alive.

Our relationship had mostly been based on sex and now that had deteriorated too, leaving us with nothing. With no sign of me getting better, and after further consultation with her family she left me.

'What a way to treat a person,' I thought, 'to be left abandoned by everyone to die and rot.'

At first I was sad but it turned into bitterness, and I blamed the doctors and my girlfriend's family for it. My resentment grew, and my hatred of everyone helped me crawl out of the hole that had been dug for me. For months after, I kept out of relationships with girls, except for a few one night stands.

It had been over a year since the collapse of my world, when I met Karen. She seemed different to the rest, and so we started going out. Very quickly she wanted to move in with me. I wasn't so keen, but eventually, mainly because I was lonely, I let her. I liked her, and she was company, but anything other than that was too much for me. All of my relationships had ended in misery, so I wasn't about to let anyone get close to me. I was cold and hard inside, and the more she tried to get near me, the more I pushed her away. At times my attitude towards her was cruel as I began to resent her being there.

In spite of my poor attitude and lack of commitment she continued to stay. It was a very one-sided affair, because I continued to live my life as a single person, and almost treated her as a housekeeper. I allowed her to do much as she liked with the flat, so using money from her job, she bought new furniture. After a few months she told me that she was pregnant. My immediate reaction was one of horror and disbelief.

'You bitch, you've set me up haven't you?' I said. 'You always told me you only wanted a man so that you could have a baby. Well I don't believe it's mine.'

'Please, you must believe me, it is yours,' she cried.

'I don't need this aggro in my life. Get out and stay out,' I said, as I forced her out the door. Later that night after I'd cooled off, I fetched her from work and let her back in. Living in the same place together became unbearable, so eventually she moved out and returned to her parents.

We continued our strange relationship at weekends in the hope that in time we might be able to repair it. After spending Christmas together, I began to have a change of heart about the pregnancy. As the date got nearer for the baby to be born, I'd fully accepted to the idea of being a father. The relationship with Karen had improved enough for us to agree to set up home together after the birth. For the first time in my life, I was actually looking forward to something. My excitement grew as the day of the birth arrived.

At the hospital the nurses sent me home as they said nothing was going to happen for another day. Unfortunately the baby was born an hour after I left. The next day I went to see them, to find a beautiful baby girl. My emotions were beginning to be churned up, as I loved her the moment I set eyes on her. It was simply amazing to be holding someone so tiny and precious that was a part of me.

We named our daughter Leoni, and she became the first and only love in my life. Her birth started to make up for some of the misery, that had dominated my life. Sadly any happiness that I was experiencing didn't last long after Karen came out of hospital. She wasn't sure what she wanted, so she took Leoni to live at her parents house and I ended up with a part-time family. The times they were with me were great as fatherhood was so rewarding.

However this temporary arrangement was doomed to failure as we grew further apart. The gaps between visits grew longer and my heart began to sink. Once again I knew I was on the receiving end of more misery. Then Karen told me she was going to stay with a friend in North Wales.

To begin with I didn't give much thought to her going, but after four weeks had passed without news, I began to worry. It felt as if all her family were ganging up on me because none of them would tell me where my daughter was. Eventually I had a phone call and my patience snapped.

'When are you coming back?' I said, angrily.

'Don't start shouting, or I may never come back,' said Karen calmly.

'Why are you doing this to me?' I asked. 'You can't just take Leoni away from me.'

'The more you go on, the less chance you've got of seeing her. Now you know what it's like don't you,' she said, hanging up the phone. I was filled with anger and despair. I longed for the day when I could hold my baby in my arms once more. The pain in my heart increased each day, as I began to think that I wouldn't see Leoni again. Then just as I was almost out of my mind with worry, they turned up.

Karen and Leoni came back to stay at the flat for a few days, and once again I began to believe that her past behaviour was over. At the weekend Karen went to her parents, but told me that when she returned it would be for good. A few days later I rang her up to find out how they both were.

'When are you coming back?' I asked.

'Never!' came her reply.

Quickly I became heated and in anger said, 'What are you going on about? I wish you would stop messing me around.'

'Look, I've found somebody else who I want to be with,' she said.

'What about Leoni? I'm her Dad.'

'I'll let you see her from time to time, and one day I'll tell her who her dad is.'

'You're winding me up, well I'm not gonna bite to that,' I said.

'Seriously Brian, get it through your head, I mean it.'

I was too stunned to reply as the message sank in, so I just hung up. The rejection bore deep inside me, worse than ever before. Not only was I being dumped, but pushed out of my daughter's life. 'I can't handle this alone,' I thought. I had to get drunk and stoned quickly to try to blot it out.

I got a bottle of valium out of the cupboard, and took a handful with a stiff drink. I emptied the rest into my pocket so I could take them down the pub without being noticed. I started to try to drown my sorrows in strong lager with brandy chasers. The valium mixed easily with the booze and it soon began to take effect.

A dark depression closed itself over me as I began to think about my little baby girl. To think that another man was probably going to take my place as her dad. All I would ever get, would be a few brief moments in the park, or a card and photograph at Christmas.

I had struggled to stay alive these last couple of years and for what, just to be put in more torment. 'Well, no more,' I said,'I'm going to put an end to this misery.'

All that effort before had taken everything out of me, and now I had nothing left. I sat in the corner alone with my booze. Taking a handful of pills from my pocket, I dropped them in my drink. I repeated the process until all the drink and pills were gone.

I left just before closing time, my intention was to get home and die. I had been out for four hours and the drink and drug cocktail was beginning to have it's sleepy effect on me. As I neared home, I came to my mate's house. In a desperate attempt for someone to show me concern or compassion, I knocked at his door.

'Do you know what I've done?' I asked. 'I've topped myself.'

'You'll be all right, go home and sleep it off,' came his reply. I left, realising there was no one I could count as my friend. Even this guy whose life I'd saved a couple of years earlier, refused to help me when it was my turn. This only added to my despair of the human race and my determination to finish myself off.

So here I sit alone in my darkness, with another failure behind me. The bitterness of the past remains to haunt me. Some strange twist of fate keeping me alive, what for, who can tell? All my strength and passion had gone into trying to take my life, so I felt unable to try again.

'All I can do is to sit awhile,' I thought. 'Take another drink, and wait and see what tomorrow brings, who knows, maybe tomorrow won't come.' I hoped it wouldn't, as every day I'd lived had been a nightmare since my childhood.

Chapter Two

TEARAWAY

During my early years as a child, we lived on the outskirts of a small country village, in Wiltshire. I was the second eldest, in a family of five children, four boys, and one girl. Both my parents worked, my mother in a hospital as a nurse, and my father as a mechanic at his garage. We never experienced a proper family life, as children and parents or as brothers and sisters.

My mother was usually depressed, or too busy to notice us, and we only ever saw our father at night. This was when the house came to life, in the shape of a terrifying violent war between my parents. It always started off in the same way in the kitchen, behind closed doors. The violence was always heard but not always seen, which made it worse.

I would sit crouching at the top of the stairs, wondering whether one or the other would be killed. I knew that as long as they were both downstairs and the row continued, I was safe. It was the silence after the row I feared the most.

When I was about seven years old the threats of violence began to include me. Many times I feared for my life, after we were told that we would all be killed. One night after a row, my dad crept upstairs and threatened me with a knife. I froze with fear at the sight of the blade, it's edge glinting menacingly. The sheets on my bed were pulled away and cut to shreds before my eyes. This time it was only a threat, but I had no way of knowing if or when I would be next.

For four years we were subject to the same kind of terror. Every night when I went to bed I couldn't sleep for fear of not waking up again. It finally came to an end when my mother tried to kill herself and was put in hospital.

After she recovered from her illness, she started working nights, so we hardly saw her. On her night off she would go to bingo with two neighbours. When I was ten I was allowed to go too.

From our house to the village was about a mile. The journey was along an unlit narrow lane which passed by a wood. It was always after 9.00pm when we left the bingo hall to walk home, so it was creepier than ever.

One night on the way home, a neighbour suggested I cut through the woods with him. He was a friend of both my parents, but especially my mother. During her illness he prevented her from throwing herself in the canal.

'We'll get home before everyone else and surprise them,' he said.

'Alright,' I said, thinking it might be fun. We stopped to share some sweets when we reached the other side of the wood. As I held out my hands to take them, he grabbed me and pulled me to the ground. For a moment I thought it was a game, but I soon realised it wasn't as he pulled my trousers down and began to assault me. His hand covered my mouth and nose, to stop me from crying out. I began to kick and struggle but he tightened his grip. After the ordeal was over he threatened to kill me if I told anyone.

'No one is gonna believe you anyway,' he said. 'I saved your mum from killing herself, so I'm a hero.'

My parents didn't even know I existed, so trying to tell them was pointless. The following week it happened again and carried on for several months.

Many times I wanted to tell someone, but there was no one I could trust. Eventually when I moved up to comprehensive school, the threats and assaults stopped.

In spite of my turbulent life at home, my grades at school were quite high. A good education was very important to me, I saw it as my ticket to a good job. At the end of term all the pupils from my year, which numbered four hundred, assembled in the main hall. We had to fill in a form stating which subjects we wanted to do the following year for our exams.

From childhood I had always been interested in writing books and wanted a career in journalism. The only suitable subjects apart from English, were Typing and Commerce, so I put them down. It was now 1972. Boys and girls still had to do traditional male and female subjects. It was unthinkable for a boy to want to do cookery, or a girl to do woodwork.

The Headmaster was walking round glancing at pupils forms, when he stopped at my desk and picked up my paper. After reading it through he turned to me, his face expressing horror.

'What's the meaning of this?' he said, waving my form around.

'I want to be a writer Sir,' I replied.

'Don't be so foolish Boy,' he shouted angrily, 'you can't do them.'

'But sir, I need them,' I pleaded. 'They're the only subjects on the list that'll help with journalism.'

Then to my horror, he held up my paper and read it out to the other pupils. 'Russ here,' he said, pointing towards me, 'wants to do typing and commerce. As you all should know, these are girls subjects only. Any normal boy would never dream of doing a subject meant for girls. I hope I won't find any other boys like him.'

It seemed like all four hundred kids were laughing at me. It was so awful, I wanted the ground to open up and swallow me. It made me feel dirty and ashamed, as if there was something unclean about me. I was taunted very badly. Fortunately for me, there were only a few days to go before the summer holidays.

During the summer, I managed to get a job working for a builder renovating council houses. In spite of being only fourteen, the men on the site treated me as a mate. On Saturday nights, all the guys went out together on a pub crawl. Because I worked alongside them, they invited me to go with them. We started off on pints of beer, and finally ended up on Pernod. It was easy to drink because it tasted so nice, but I was unaware how strong it was. As I was under age the guy's told me to say I was a jockey because they always looked young. In one pub we had to put the story to the test, when a barmaid asked me my age.

'I'm nineteen,' I said confidently.

'You don't look nineteen to me,' she said.

'I am, honest,' I said, trying to look innocent. 'I'm a jockey from the local riding stables, and I'm always having this problem.'

She fell for it, but I nearly came unstuck when one of the customers asked me for a tip. Quickly I made up some names and race meetings, and somehow I got away with it. We all had a laugh at the thought of him trying to place a bet on a bogus horse.

I came home drunk and very late, but no one seemed to notice. From then on, I spent every Saturday night drinking with my new mates.

The start of a new school term came quicker than I'd hoped. I was dreading going back to school, as I was sure the kids would remember the Headmaster's comments about me. With this in mind I decided to play truant.

At first I started by bunking off after registration, so they would think I was having a free period. Eventually as that got harder to do, I stopped going altogether. There were several truancy officers in our area, so I had to be careful not to be seen. For a lot of the time, I stayed on the canal towpath to keep out of the way. It became a lonely existence, but that was much better than being hounded at school. To survive the isolation, I would sometimes visit the cafe and play on the fruit machines. To do this I had to have money, and also not to look like I was skipping school.

I overcame looking like a schoolboy by wearing a pair of overalls over my uniform. As time went by, I managed to convince most of the people in the cafe that I was working.

To keep myself in money I stole from home, phone boxes and anywhere else I could find. As my need grew for cigarettes, drinking and gambling, I began robbing houses and stealing from cars. I became a regular visitor to the second hand shop, with things to sell. I still had a part-time job with the builder. In the evenings, for a couple of hours he would let me do odd jobs in his workshop. After work, I would meet up with some older lads who I had got to know at the cafe. We often spent the evenings drinking beer and cider, which we stole from the back of the brewery.

After months of constant truanting I was found out. The education officer was at our house almost every day. Never once was I asked if there was anything wrong, or why I played truant. Nothing he threatened me with ever made a difference, as I continued to bunk off school. Finally I was told that I would be sent to a home for awkward boys unless I complied with his wishes.

Our neighbours sympathised with my parents, saying they didn't deserve such a horrid child. I was made to feel that I was to blame for all the rows that had ever taken place. It was very hard to take, to see my whole family against me. I felt so depressed I thought about killing myself, but instead I decided to run away from home. In the dark of the night I left, taking only a few stolen pounds and some sandwiches. By chance a lorry driver I knew was going to Cambridge to deliver a load of chickens, so I scrounged a lift with him. He told me he would be gone a couple of days, and if I wanted to come back with him, I could. He kept me supplied with cigarettes and food in return for help in unloading his lorry.

'Will you get into trouble if I don't come back?' I asked.

'I might,' he said, 'but don't worry about that.'

I didn't want to get him in trouble, so I returned home with him. It was late when I returned, so I crept indoors hoping everyone was asleep. As I reached the top of the stairs, my dad came out of his room. I stood still, waiting expectantly for him to shout at me. Instead there was deathly silence. It was as though I wasn't there.

The police arrived the next morning, to take me to school. They had been out searching for me the day before. Teachers and children alike stared at the police car, trying to get a look at who was inside. Although it was a bit embarrassing, it was quite exciting too. For a few days I stayed in my classes, because the police were still keeping a check on me. However my education meant nothing to me now, so I refused to take part in the lessons.

One morning during the French lesson, I finally boiled over when the teacher continued to harass me.

'Russ, will you please read your text book,' said a red-faced teacher.

'I'll sit here, but I'm not taking part,' I said.

'You'll do as I say,' she said poking me. 'Now get on with your work!'

'Have your books,' I said, as I shoved them at her, knocking her down.

Two teachers arrived from other rooms as I was walking out. 'Where are you going boy?' said one.

'Away from you lot forever,' I said angrily. 'You and your precious school can get lost.' I could hear them shouting at me to come back, but it was too late, as I had already reached the exit. I was really pleased with myself as a letter was sent to my parents informing them of my expulsion.

Fortunately being expelled didn't stop me getting a job, as I quickly started work on a pig farm. It didn't take me long to learn the job or get to know the adult boars. They soon responded to my voice and greeted me every morning as I arrived for work. I often spent long periods of time talking to them. My relationship with them was much better than it ever was with people. They were very clean and intelligent animals and responded well to any kindness shown to them. The boars were reared from the farmers own stock, so I knew some of them from birth. One of them in particular called Bill was my favourite, and he soon became my best friend.

Letting the boars run with the sows to mate was always a dangerous and delicate job. The boars had to be kept apart at all times, otherwise they would fight to the death. Unfortunately one day two boars accidently ended up together in the passageway.

Bill was one, and the other was called George. They both weighed around 400lb, and all of it solid muscle. Their jaws were so powerful they could tear a man's arm right off. George had an advantage over Bill; four large tusks, which hung outside his mouth.

The fight was set, like two boxers in a ring. They circled around, each eyeing the other up. Then the battle commenced as the two beasts attacked each other. It was a frightening sight, and the noise was just like dogs fighting. The manager and I raced to the scene to try and separate them, but it was too late. Bill's rear had been torn open by George's ferocious tusks. He was losing a lot of blood, and could no longer stand as the wound opened up some more. Bill wanted to stop fighting. He looked like a defeated opponent as he tried desperately to get away. Sensing blood and victory, George went in for the kill.

We tried to stun him by throwing water over him but it had no effect. I felt helpless, unable to do anything but watch one animal slaughter the other. I was angry at George as he was trying to kill Bill who was my friend. I felt guilty because it was partly my fault this had happened. I picked up a piece of wood and hit George across the head, but he just knocked it from my hand.

In a last desperate attempt I went in with boots flying. Punching and kicking him continually in the head until he eventually staggered backwards. A few blows had struck him in the nose which is a pigs sensitive area, but it was more luck than anything else. With a space now between them, I was able to drive George away. Bill had been seriously hurt, but with a lot of stitches and care he recovered.

Bill became much gentler afterwards, and was always first to greet me in the morning. On most days, I would sit next to him in his pen and eat my lunch. This huge beast was a potential killer, yet never once did I feel threatened.

Even though I was fairly happy at work, the rest of my life was still awful. The evenings at home were unbearable, so I spent every night in the pub. The drink helped me to cope, and it quickly became very important to me. My work began to be affected by my drunkeness as I started to turn up late every day. Finally after repeated warnings, I lost my job.

After many months of being broke, I turned to robbery. I knew of an elderly farmer who lived with his sisters. They all lived together in a remote farmhouse, a mile from the village. It was an easy target, as every Sunday without fail they would go to church. Each week while they were out, I would sneak in and take ten or fifteen pounds from their home. They always had hundreds of pounds hidden in the house, so I knew they wouldn't notice it missing. However the temptation to take all their money eventually got the better of me. The opportunity came when I got a job working on a travelling-fair. The weekend the fair moved away from the area I went with it, taking all the farmer's money with me.

Chapter Three

THE FAIRGROUND

The glamour of working on the fair always attracted me. As a spectator I had often admired the men working on it. They gave the impression of being tough, adventurous and without fear. It was like watching film stars acting, as they jumped on and off the fast moving rides. However when the fair was shut, it soon lost it's attraction. The putting up and taking down of the fair wasn't as glamorous, especially when it was raining.

I started work on the bumper cars along with three other guys. Our wages were poor, but all our meals and accommodation were included. On our fairground, each ride had it's own caravan. But other rides that sometimes travelled with us weren't so lucky. Workers slept all year round in lorry cabs or box-trucks.

Going from town to town made it easy to pick up girls. Often they hung around the ride waiting to be chatted up. Most of us had a different girl in every town, and sometimes more than one. Sex played a major part in the role of a fairground worker. If you didn't score with the girls, you were seen very much as a failure. By now I had a regular girlfriend who came to every town I was in. Sometimes she would turn up unexpectedly, which could be awkward especially if I was with another girl.

With rare exceptions Sunday was our day off. We generally finished work at lunchtime, after we had moved towns. In the afternoon we tried to catch up on lost sleep, but by six thirty we were washed and ready to go out. Before we got our weekly pay, we received the usual Sunday night lecture from the boss.

'No fighting, and don't drink too much,' he said.

'Yes boss,' we all shouted. As soon as we were away from the ground, we all started laughing at our boss. He knew it was useless to ask us to behave, but he'd got into the habit of saying it. Most Sunday's we were involved in some disturbance or another. Generally it was our fault, but occasionally we were innocent.

Because of our poor wages, we had to use various cons and other ways of deception to subsidise them. Off the ground we would take on the locals in anything to make a quid. A drinking challenge was one of these games of chance. Paddy was our champion, and he was practically unbeatable in a drinking competition. He could drink a pint of lager in under three seconds. Somehow he managed to keep his throat open so that he swallowed continuously. We offered good odds for anyone who could beat him. Wherever we went there was never any shortage of takers.

'Who's next,' I said, after Paddy won his first contest.

'I'll tell you what,' Paddy said. 'I'll put my pint on the floor and pick it up in my teeth to drink it.'

Such a show of arrogance was enough to capture another few mugs. We put on this show in different pubs, across several counties and never lost once. On or off the ground, life was never boring. But sometimes it could be quite frightening, especially when several hundred people came onto the ground for a fight. It was also quite dangerous to go back to some of the towns we'd visited. There were always plenty of people with one grudge or another. Either you'd kicked someones head in or pinched someone else's girlfriend. Twice in Salisbury, I was involved in an affray over these things.

One night after the pubs had shut, I was going to the chippy with my mate Terry, who worked on the Waltzer. The chip shop entrance was partially blocked by some scaffolding, so there was only room for one person at a time to pass. As we got there two squaddies came out and barred our way, so angrily I pushed one of them to the ground.

'You'd better apologise to him,' said a blonde-headed guy, pointing to his mate on the floor.

'Clear off, you idiot,' I snarled back at him.

He turned his attention to Terry who suddenly hit him. I went to grab the guy who had been on the floor, but he ran off into the chip shop. In the struggle, Terry slipped and fell backwards towards the scaffolding. In an attempt to stop him from hitting his head, I put my arm out to catch him. As I did, a blow from an iron bar struck my head, knocking me off balance. Straightening up, I threw a punch towards my attacker, but instead of hitting him, I was hit again in the eye. Bang Bang, as another two blows came crashing into my face. Remarkably I was still standing upright, although I had difficulty in focusing.

'What's keeping him up?' I heard one of them shout.

'He's not human is he?' shouted another. Then two or three more blows hit me, and I crashed to the floor and blacked out.

When I came round they had gone, and we were surrounded by police. An ambulance arrived and we were taken to the hospital. Terry had sustained a broken neck, while I looked like I'd been in a collision with a bus.

According to witnesses, there were five of them, all armed with short bars from the scaffolding. Although I had been beaten up in the fight, it brought me respect as a tough guy for being able withstand it.

At the start of the next season I began working on the Waltzer with Terry. This gave me wider opportunities, as we travelled further. During the summer our rides travelled around the coastal towns with another fair. There was a guy from Liverpool, called Scouse, who worked on the Cyclone Twist. We became good mates, and when we parted agreed to meet up at the end of the season. Winter soon came, and we met up at the fairground yard on the outskirts of Devizes, as arranged.

Neither of us had anywhere to live, so we slept in one of the empty caravans. Most of the owners spent the winter at home or on holiday, so we weren't noticed. Scouse was about thirty, almost twelve years older than me, and had been in prison several times. He taught me everything he knew about committing robberies, and soon I was as good as he was. After a few months of success we decided to take a break, as the police were getting closer. Scouse had friends and relations in Liverpool, so we decided to go there for a while.

'I know someone we can stay with for a while,' said Scouse. 'He's a disc jockey, and he lives and works around Merseyside, he'll put us up.' We left the next day, and caught the express train to Liverpool.

I had never been on a train before, or even to a big city, so it was an exciting adventure. As the train pulled into Lime Street station, I was amazed at the size of the crowds. Stepping onto the platform was an achievement in itself, as the crowds of people pushed and shoved each other. We caught the next train to Warrington, where Scouse had arranged for us to meet his mates. At Warrington station, we met Tommy, one of Scouse's mates, who took us to a place called the Wilderspool club. There at the back of the club we met the disc-jockey Mick. He had agreed to let us stay at his house, until we found somewhere more permanent.

During the disco on the way back from the toilets, I accidently entered a private room. Inside there was a bar and a snooker table, with six or seven men around it. As they turned round to see who it was coming in, their jackets opened and I saw two of them wearing guns.

'What do you want kid?' said a burly looking man.

'Nothing,' I said nervously, 'I just took a wrong turn.'

'Then turn around and beat it,' he said with a snarl. They watched me closely as I edged myself slowly back out of the door.

Towards the end of the evening, the big, burly chap came into the disco, along with two others. As they walked around, I watched in admiration as everyone moved respectfully from their path.

When we had packed up the disco equipment and were leaving, I told Mick and Scouse what I had seen.

'That's where the local underworld hangs out,' said Mick. 'I should keep quiet about that if I were you.'

On the way to Wigan, Mick started talking about his pets. 'I'm into reptiles in a big way,' he said. 'In fact I've got two snakes at home. One young boa-constrictor and Oscar, my python.'

'I always thought you were a weirdo,' said Scouse, laughing.

'Do you like snakes Brian? ' asked Mick.

'No, I don't,' I said, 'they're creepy.'

'I keep them locked up,' he said calmly. 'Well, most of the time anyway.'

'What do you mean most of the time?' said Scouse, looking worried.

'Oscar's only got out the once,' said Mick. 'He must've escaped when I was taking his dinner in.'

'Where does he live then?' I asked.

'In one of the bedrooms, of course,' said Mick, in amazement.

'You got him back then?' said Scouse.

'Oh yeah, I found him a week later, in the next door neighbours garden. The only thing was their scotty dog went missing the same day as Oscar did, and hasn't been seen since.

'You don't think he ate him, do you?' asked Scouse.

'Most definitely,' said Mick, grinning.

'Why does it have to be snakes?' I said, quietly to myself. Snakes were my biggest phobia. As a child I had nightmares about them, after getting too close to an adder.

We arrived at Mick's house and started unloading the van into his lounge. As I went in, I found that Mick had been telling the truth about his pets, because there in a glass tank, was the boa-constrictor. As I brought the last piece of equipment in, I was met by Mick holding the snake in his hand.

'I thought you said it was only young,' I said, taking a couple of steps backwards.

'He is,' said Mick, 'he's still only eight feet long.'

'Only,' said Scouse, 'well I'd hate to meet him when he grows up.'

Mick started to kiss it, and then he brought it over to me. 'Give him a kiss,' said Mick, thrusting the snake into my face. 'He's been on his own all day.'

The sight of his fangs flickering in and out, was the last straw. I ran out of the house and down the road.

'Where are you going,' shouted Mick after me.

'Anyplace, where that snake isn't,' I said.

'I'll put him back in his case then,' said Mick.

Slowly I crept back inside, and looked around the lounge door. With great relief, I saw that the snake was back in his case where he belonged. It was two o'clock by the time we all got to bed.

'You've got that room on the end,' said Mick. 'Don't go in the middle one because that's Oscar's.'

'You needn't worry about that,' said Scouse.

'He can't get out, can he?' I said, feeling petrified.

'No, you'll be all right, I promise,' said Mick.

Scouse and I were both scared, so we shoved a wardrobe against the door just in case.

'You can sleep next to the door Scouse,' I said, 'cause if Oscar's hungry, he can eat you first.' Neither of us slept very well, and it was a great relief when morning came.

Mick told us we were welcome to stay as long as we liked, but thankfully we had somewhere else to go. I would have slept naked on the streets before I spent another night in the snake pit.

The place we had been promised was not as we expected. It was a derelict house, without a proper door and no windows. It was near the Mersey river, and every time the wind blew the chill went right through my bones. We stuck it out for a while, but sleeping rough in the middle of winter was no joke.

Finally the cold got the better of us, and we returned to Wiltshire. We soon started robbing again, but this time we weren't so lucky. Within a short while I was behind bars in a Detention Centre. Every night in my cell, I thought of the gangsters from Liverpool, and dreamed of becoming one myself.

Chapter Four

RAGING BULL

After my release from the Detention Centre, I went back home to live with my parents. However the peace in the house was soon shattered with my heavy drinking and fighting. At least once a week the police were at our door for one thing or another. Finally after a furious row, I left and moved in with my girlfriend from the fairground.

Our relationship was a stormy one most of the time, yet in spite of this we were inseparable. One Saturday night outside our local pub, we were having a blazing row. As it heated up she pushed me, making me fall over the bonnet of a parked car. Unknown to us, a police van had just pulled up with two coppers in it.

'What's going on here then?' said one of them, coming over.

'Nothing, he's just fallen over,' said my girlfriend.

Before anything else was said, the two coppers had dragged me to the van and were shoving me inside.

'Leave him alone,' screamed my girlfriend.

'Get lost,' said the youngest cop, throwing her to the ground.

Suddenly I went berserk and picked up the copper and threw him into the road. Within minutes I was going on the rampage, punching and smashing everything in sight. My temper deepened and my mind went blank, as police reinforcements arrived. The next thing I knew I was lying face down in an army Landrover handcuffed. I managed to move my head enough so that I could see who my captors were. There were four MPs, as well as several coppers. When we got to the nick I was carried down the corridor to the cell block.

'Boy, this guy's hard to get hold of,' said one cop, as he and others struggled to get me locked up.

I managed to get free from their grasp and ran to the other end of the cell block.

'You've had it now you nutter,' they all shouted, taking out their truncheons.

I was still handcuffed as they began their assault upon me. Blow after blow struck me around the head and chest, as their frenzied attack increased.

I roared in anger and struck out like a cornered animal, knocking one copper to the floor. 'Come on who's next,' I screamed, 'I'll do the lot of you.'

Just as they were about to rush me again, the sergeant came in. 'What the hell's going on,' he barked loudly, as he threw himself between us.

'Don't you know what he's done?' said one of them. 'Some of our mates are in casualty because of him.'

'I'm well aware of what's happened,' he said, 'but let's do things right. Now get those cuffs off, and get out.'

'I'm not going near him,' said the officer, 'he's a Psycho.'

'Yeah that's right,' agreed another, 'he needs certifying.'

'Give me the keys then,' ordered the sergeant. 'I've known him since he was a kid, so I'll be all right.'

'Rather you than me sarge,' said the officer, 'but I still think he ought to be in a strait-jacket.

All the others left, leaving me alone with the sergeant.

'You know me, don't you Brian? It's Sergeant Brown. I used to be your village bobby. Now I'm just going to take off those handcuffs, and then you can get cleaned up.'

I held out my arms, watching him closely as he took the handcuffs off. It was a relief to get them off, because they had tightened during the struggle.

'I'll just go and get you some cigarettes,' he said, disappearing out of the door.

I sat down and slumped up against the wall. My breathing was rapid and my mind was racing. As I started to come to terms with my surroundings the sergeant returned with the cigarettes.

'What am I doing here,' I asked, jumping up.

'Just calm down,' he said, 'we'll talk later.

'Calm down,' I screamed, 'I've been beaten and put in the nick, and for what.'

'You'll have to cool off first, or else I'll call the doctor. At the rate you're going you'll burst a blood-vessel, or worse.'

He locked the gate and dissappeared once again, leaving me to my rage. I sat back down on the floor, and put my head in my hands. The night's events had started to take it's toll on me, as exhaustion began to eat into my strength. When I had calmed down, I began to examine myself for injuries.

My hands were caked with blood, mostly from the torn skin on my wrists where the cuffs had been. My clothes resembled rags. My jumper was torn at the sleeve and my shirt looked like it had been through a shredder.

Once I started to clean myself up, the extent of my injuries became clearer. A stabbing pain shot through my chest as I took off the ragged shirt. Both sides of my ribcage was black with bruising, from all the blows I'd received.

'How long have I been here,' I wondered, as my senses began to return.

It was like I was waking up out of a deep sleep after a dream. Except this wasn't a dream but a nightmare. My head throbbed as I tried frantically to recall what had happened. It was hopeless; my mind had gone blank. My thoughts were interrupted by the sergeant returning.

'Right then Brian, are you feeling better?' he asked. 'Let's see if we can't resolve this little matter.'

'Tell me, what was I doing in an army truck?' I asked.

'We couldn't handle you alone,' he said, 'so we asked the MPs to help us.'

'I can't remember much before then, except I didn't start it.'

'Now I've charged you with being drunk and disorderly,' he said ignoring my reply. On Monday morning you'll go to court, but I shouldn't think it'll take long.'

'I wasn't drunk,' I said protesting, 'and I was only disorderly because your lot picked on me.'

'Brian, I'm doing you a favour,' he said. 'At least five officers were hurt in the fight with you, so really that's assault.'

'I was just defending myself,' I replied.

'I don't think they would see it like that,' he said. 'If you want my advice you'll cut your losses, and plead guilty to the charges I've given you.'

'I'll think about it,' I said, 'but I still think it's a stitch up.'

'Before you go, there's just one more thing, an appointment has been made for you to see a psychiatrist.'

'You're joking, what the hell for, I'm no nut.'

'It's up to you,' said the sergeant shrugging his shoulders, 'but next time you lose your temper you might kill someone.'

By the time I finally left the police station it was 11.30am the following day. As it was almost opening time at the pub, I went straight there.

When I arrived, my attention was drawn to a crowd of people standing by a skip at the side of the pub. I peered over the shoulder of the person in front of me, to see two men trying to move a large block of stone.

'That lunatic Brian Russ had this above his head last night,' said Jacko, one of the men struggling with the stone.

'Do you want a hand?' I said grinning.

'Oh hello Brian,' said Jacko nervously, 'I didn't see you there.'

'You don't expect me to believe that I lifted that up do you?' I said.

'Not only lift it, but you threw it at the police,' said Billy, the other man by the stone.

I helped them heave it into the skip, and went into the pub as it opened.

'I'm gasping for a pint,' I said to the landlord. 'I never got to finish the one I had last night.'

'Your money's no good in here today Bri,' he said, 'nor for a while I fancy.'

'Sorry, but I haven't a clue what you're talking about,' I said.

'The whole pub was outside watching you beat the police up last night. You're a celebrity now mate, everyone will want to shake your hand and buy you a drink.'

'Listen, I wish someone would tell me what happened,' I said, 'because I can't remember a thing.'

'Fancy becoming famous and not knowing how it happened,' laughed Harry the barman.

'You're funny I don't think,' I said, getting annoyed. I sat down with Billy and Jacko as they began to give an account of the nights events.

'We saw one copper fall into the road, as you burst out from the back of the police van,' stated Jacko. 'Then you ran across the road and jumped on his mate.'

'It wasn't long before the area was swarming with coppers,' said Billy exagerating, 'well a dozen at least.'

'I don't think it would have made any difference how many their were,' said Jacko.

Suddenly the bar went quiet as two local toughs walked in and approached me. They were a lot older than me, and were respected and feared by most of the community. Everyone gave a sigh of relief as they had only come to offer me their respect.

'When the MPs arrived I thought their was going to be a full scale riot,' said Jacko continuing. 'They joined forces with the police and started battering you with their batons.'

'We were cheering you on though Bri,' said Harry. 'The more they hit you, the more you fought them off.'

'Yeah, you're my hero,' said Billy. 'I hate the pigs, and anyone who can take them on single handed is great in my book.'

'Everyone's talking about you,' said Billy. 'Some people have even started calling you Psycho, and Animal. I reckon you could just about do what you like now.'

'Billy's right you know, no one will dare cross you they'll be too frightened, said Harry.

'I think I'll wait until after I've been to court tomorrow before I celebrate,' I said, as I left. Walking home, I felt ten feet tall as I pondered on my new status as the town tough.

The night passed quickly, and soon I was standing on the steps outside the court. The room went quiet as I breezed through the large court doors. Very quickly I was ushered into the courtroom, and stood before the bench.

For a while I disputed the charge, but after legal advice I pleaded guilty and was fined £50. However the magistrates warned me severely to seek help for my aggressive behaviour. I walked out of the court feeling superior to everyone else, and gloated at the disgruntled faces of the law.

Back on the streets, the story of my single-handed battle with the police carried on being told. I decided going to the psychiatric clinic would further my reputation as well as keeping the cops off my back.

'I'd better watch out what I say,' I thought, while I waited outside the psychiatrists office.' One wrong word, and I might never see the outside world again.'

A nurse showed me into a room where two strange looking men in white coats were waiting for me.

'I'm Doctor White, and this is my colleague Doctor Baker. Now I understand you're having a few problems.'

'I haven't got a problem, it's everybody else mate.'

'You can't carry on losing your temper,' said Dr Baker, 'especially when you get so violent.'

'Tell me, do you hear voices or see things?' said Dr White.

'Of course I hear voices who doesn't,' I said, getting angry. 'As for seeing things, only when I'm drunk.'

'How much would you say you drank?'

'Quite a lot, I like drinking, it's one of my best friends and it never answers me back.'

'Do you feel that drinking makes you more likely to be aggressive, or helps you relax.'

'What is this twenty questions?' I shouted. 'Are you sure you're not a copper? I'll tell you the reason, it's because people like you never know when to stop pushing me. Well the next time someone does they'll be sorry.'

I was getting quite angry with being questioned, so I got up and left, slamming the door behind me. Walking through the grounds of the clinic, I swore I'd never return.

However it wasn't too long before I was back, after my girlfriend left me during a lengthy illness. But after months of getting bored I gave up going, and turned to drugs instead.

I moved into a new flat in a different neighbourhood. It was there I met Karen who was to become the mother of my daughter Leoni. It wasn't long before she was moving in and starting to plan the future.

Unfortunately we both had different ideas, Karen wanted a nice home, while I hungered for power and a bigger reputation.

Chapter Five

REVENGE

My time at the psychiatric clinic had brought a new meaning to my reputation. Whenever I was challenged, I would enter the fight with a view to destroy my opponent. If I got beat I would lose everything, so my motto was to kill or be killed.

I became obsessed with weapons especially knives, and regularly carried more than one. Although the police still feared me, it didn't stop them trying to nick me. Many times I was interviewed over stabbings and assaults, but never charged.

I started to feel above the law, as people were too afraid to give evidence against me. This only made my fantasy of being a Gangster even more real. A few months later I started to get involved in drug dealing and extortion.

I formed a gang with an old schoolmate called Geordie who had moved into our neighbourhood. Soon fast cars and guard dogs became a common sight on our estate.

It wasn't long before the other residents on the estate started to complain about us. Most of the time we ignored them, but when they tried to have us evicted we retaliated. The damage we inflicted to vehicles and homes, soon put a stop to their complaints.

However one neighbour called Glover wasn't so easily shaken. He was about forty and he lived alone in the next block of flats to me. Although I disliked him intensely, he had his usefulness. He was unemployed and in need of cash, so I used him in a robbery, hoping to gain a hold over him.

After a successful raid on a club we drove to the motorway services near Chippenham for breakfast. While we were there I was approached by a policeman who said I was under arrest for armed robbery at Aust services.

'You're off your rocker mate,' I said, pushing him to the ground, and walking off.

'You wont get away,' he shouted after me.

'That copper's a nutter,' said Geordie, 'he didn't even know our names.'

'With any luck, that's the way it'll stay too,' I said.

We turned off the motorway, and drove down the country lanes to avoid detection. It had been snowing for several days, so the roads were quite bad. Suddenly I lost control of the car as it slid about on the ice. In a split second we were being thrown around as the car hit the bank and rolled over. Fortunately we all escaped unhurt, but sadly my car was a write off. We managed to get a lift into Chippenham, where we waited for a taxi. Before one arrived, we found ourselves surrounded by police cars coming from all directions.

We were taken to the local nick where we were detained for interrogation by Bristol detectives. While we waited for them to arrive, Glover told them about our raid, and how he was forced to take part. We were all charged with the club robbery but I was the only one who wasn't released. Bristol CID were still convinced that I was involved in the armed robbery. They tried everything to get me to admit it, even the good cop, bad cop routine. Finally they gave up, and reluctantly let me go. At court I got lucky, as the magistrates handed out suspended prison sentences for robbery.

Not long after, Karen became pregnant, and went back to live with her parents. While she was away, I decided it was time to repay Glover for his treachery. Not only did he get assaulted, but we set our dogs on his cats, killing one of them.

'That could be you Glover,' I said warning him. The look on his face told me that he'd got the message.

As the birth of our child got closer, Karen began to spend more time with me at the flat. One day when I returned home I found Glover sat on the sofa drinking coffee. He had been doing some odd jobs for one of Karen's friends, and now he was helping her. Glover smiled, as he could see I was irritated by his presence.

He became a regular visitor to our flat. Everytime I looked round, there he was grinning. I started to feel like I was an intruder in my home. My hatred grew daily, and I began to wish him dead. I tried spiking his drinks in the hope he'd get sick or worse, but that didn't work.

'He's got to go,' I said to Geordie.

Eventually I came up with a plan. Every Friday night Glover walked to the pub. He always returned along the same route, and at the same time.

One Friday Geordie and I hid along the route in the dark, as we waited for his return. It was almost midnight when he walked by us. Quickly we crept up behind him and dragged him into the shadows.

'You're a dead man,' I said, holding a bayonet tightly to his throat.

'What are you going to do?' he cried.

'It's pay back time, you creep,' said Geordie.

'Keep away from my family,' I said, pulling the blade across his throat. 'Or next time I'll take your head right off.'

We vanished into the darkness leaving him a bloody, sobbing wreck on the floor.

I thought that would be the end of the matter, but a week later I received a letter from his solicitor. It said he was suing me for damages he'd received in the car crash. I didn't have time do anything about it, because Karen gave birth to our baby daughter Leoni.

My excitement was dampened when I received notice from the courts that Glover had been awarded £1000.

'I'll have his head this time.' I said, screwing the letter up. I couldn't afford to let people think I was going soft, or else I'd lose my credibility. However I had to wait for the right opportunity, because Karen was now living with me all the time.

The tension continued to grow as Glover remained on the scene. I heard a rumour that he'd been involved in a sexual offence, but it wasn't ever proven. This gave me the ammunition I needed to keep him out of my flat, but it came too late.

When I got home from work, Karen was leaving for Wales, to stay at a friends house. She was frightened and cying as she told me of her ordeal with Glover.

'He made sexual threats towards me and Leoni,' she said.

Even after she'd locked the door, he still tried to get in. The police were contacted but refused to get involved.

Now Karen was out of the way, I could finally deal with Glover. All my previous attempts on his life had failed, but this time I would make sure. The problem was how to get to him, as he had stopped going out after my last attempt.

I got an idea of how to solve it when I arrived at the pub. Geordie and another mate called Johnno were there. They were drunk and in an aggressive mood. Suddenly the idea of using them to flush Glover out into the open struck me.

'Glover's been up to his old tricks,' I said, getting them some more drinks.

'What do you mean,' said Geordie.

'He's been spreading rumours, of how he could have you in a fight,' I said lying.

'We'll see about that,' said Johnno, getting wound up.

'Prove it then,' I said.

It only took a couple more drinks and a few more lies, to get them hooked. Soon we were on our way to Glover's flat, all desperate for his blood.

I didn't waste anytime when we arrived, for fear of them changing their minds. Quickly I smashed Glover's window, and sent Johnno in. Geordie followed him in and opened the door for me.

Before I entered his flat, I looked around at the flapping curtains in the neighbours windows. I knew they were watching me, but I didn't care. They knew from past experience what to expect if they interfered.

I went inside and closed the door behind, confident we wouldn't be disturbed. My adrenalin pumped faster, as I walked into Glover's bedroom. Then as my eyes met his I flew into a blind rage.

'Get out of my home,' he ordered.

'Shut it, you creep,' I snapped. 'You're in no position to dictate to me.

'Look if it's about the money, I'll forget the claim,' he said, getting worried.

'It's too late for that now,' I said, as I grabbed hold of him. 'Where you're going you won't need any money anyway. I warned you to stay away from my family didn't I?'

'Please, give me another chance,' he begged. 'I'll keep away.'

'You're vermin Glover, and you need exterminating,' I said. I threw him against the bedroom wall and smashed his head into it. My hands went round his throat and I began to squeeze.

'Please help me,' he spluttered.

The terror and panic in his face grew, as I tightened my grip on his throat. The feeling of power over life and death excited me, and I squeezed all the more.

'He's learnt his lesson now Bri, hasn't he?' asked Geordie.

'His kind never learn,' I said.

'You'll kill him in a minute,' said Johnno, looking worried.

Their pleas became fainter as I lost all control. My eyes were transfixed on those of my victim, watching him choke. Suddenly I lost my grip, when Geordie and Johnno pulled at me from behind.

'Leave him,' said Geordie, 'he's not worth it.'

Glover crawled into a corner and made himself as small as possible.

'You're one lucky man,' I said, pointing to Glover. 'This never happened tonight, do you understand?'

He nodded his head in agreement. 'Say it,' I shouted angrily.

'Yes, I understand,' he said nervously.

'If you blab or cross me again,' I said, 'one day I'll come back and finish you off, I promise.'

'Yeah, that's right,' said Geordie and Johnno.

'No matter where you are, I'll get you,' I said, menacingly. 'Remember this, an Englishman's home is his castle, but not for you, get it?'

'Let's go,' said Geordie already on his way out of the door. 'I'm sure he's got the message.'

We crept out closing the door behind us, and went our separate ways. It was now one o'clock in the morning, so the cover of darkness swallowed us up. Within minutes I was safely indoors, and went to bed happy and content.

Chapter Six

THE CONTEST

My confidence was soon shattered, when the police arrived at my door a few days later. There were six detectives inside the hallway of the flats. Two by my door, and the other four guarding the exits from the block. The two nearest me were DC Watts and DC Howard who I'd known for several years.

'What do you want?' I said aggressively.

'We'd like to ask you some questions about the other night,' said DC Howard.

'Other night, what other night was that?' I asked innocently.

'You know,' snarled Watts. 'The night you tried to murder Mr Glover.'

'You're off your head mate,' I said laughing. 'I reckon someone's playing a joke on you.'

Just then two more officers came into the block of flats. Howard turned and gestured to them to stay where they were.

'I'm aware of your reputation Brian,' said Howard. 'Let's hope there's no need to test it.'

Howard showed me respect, where Watts had only contempt for me. The feeling was mutual, as Watts and I had been involved in a violent struggle before.

'What do you want to know then?' I asked.

'Not here, down the nick,' said Watts getting impatient.

'Brian you don't seem to appreciate the seriousness of the allegations,' said DC Howard. 'It could even be attempted murder.'

'Fair enough, let's go then,' I said, calmly walking out the door.

I was put under arrest, although they didn't handcuff me. It wasn't long before I was being escorted off the estate. As we drove away in a convoy of four cars, the neighbours came out to see me off.

'Don't get too cosy, I'll be back,' I said under my breath.

There was a warm reception of more than a dozen coppers waiting for me in the station. I stopped briefly to give a sarcastic grin to the troops, before walking on to the cells. I chuckled to myself as they banged me up, they were obviously expecting me to struggle.

I didn't have to wait very long before the rest of the gang were in the cells. I could recognise Geordie's voice as he shouted abuse all the way to his cell. It was fairly quiet in the cell block, so we were able to talk to each other through the walls.

'What's going on,' said Geordie, 'do you think they know anything.'

'Keep your voice down and stay calm,' I said. 'They don't know anything, so just keep quiet.'

Our conversation was interupted as the cell block gate opened. The interrogation had begun, as Johnno was led away for his interview. The cell gate banged shut, and all was quiet again. I started pacing the floor and thinking about what would be said. Having been so confident that no one would talk, we forgot to establish an alibi.

The noise of the cell gate opening put a halt to my thoughts, as Geordie was exchanged for Johnno. I couldn't find out what Johnno had said, because he was too far away to be heard.

It was eleven o'clock when the gate opened again and they marched Geordie back. I got up expecting my cell to open, but they just shut the gate and walked off.

Another hour of constant worry passed by, before they came and took me to the interview room. Inside, DC Watts and Howard were sat at a desk whispering to each other. I sat down and waited for the contest to begin.

DC Howard leaned forward and asked me the first question. 'On Tuesday night Mr Glover says you forced your way into his home and tried to murder him. What do you say in response to this allegation?'

I shrugged my shoulders, and just told them he must have been mistaken.

'We've seen his injuries and the damage to his home, how do you account for that?'

'Who knows,' I said, 'maybe he fell over.'

'Mr Glover said he's been awarded £1000 damages against you,' said Howard. 'The court pays him, and you pay them, do you agree?'

'Yes there was a claim,' I replied.

'Is it true that you made a threat to Mr.Glover telling him he wouldn't live to spend it?'

'No that's total rubbish.'

'May I suggest to you that Tuesday night you attempted to carry out your threat,' said Howard confidently.

'You can suggest anything you like, but it's all lies,' I said defiantly.

Howard opened a file and took out a piece of paper. It was a list of complaints which had all come from our neighbourhood. My name was mentioned on every one and he wanted to know why? I told them I thought it was because they were from a different age group, and were jealous of my lifestyle. I also mentioned that I was a victim of a malicious campaign to have me evicted.

'Our information is that they are the victims of your terror campaign against them,' said Howard. 'Some people have moved out of their homes for fear of attacks.'

I was getting tired and my answers were getting shorter. I was beginning to regret not having my solicitor present.

'Do you have any weapons, like a gun or bayonet perhaps?' said Howard. 'Remember we can get a search warrant and check.'

I put my head in my hands, and gently rubbed my eyes. I knew I had to be careful how I answered, I didn't need them snooping around at home.

'Yes I've got a bayonet,' I said. 'So what, there's no law saying I can't have one is there ?'

'That depends on what you've got it for,' said DC Watts sarcastically.

'Mr. Glover says he's seen your bayonet up real close. In fact he told us you tried to cut his throat with it.'

'You don't really believe that creep, do you?' I asked. 'I can't believe you're that gullible.'

'Listen Brian,' said Watts, 'I've seen a lot of people come in here and make up stories. This is one of the few cases that I believe to be genuine. He was that scared, he wanted us to put him in protective custody.'

'Am I supposed to be impressed by that,' I said, not caring.

Suddenly Watts got up and shoved his chair towards the wall. His face was red and he looked like thunder. I wondered if this was a new tactic or for real. He came towards me and grabbed me by my shirt and started poking me in the chest. 'Stop messing us about,' said Watts seething with rage.

'Don't touch me copper, or you'll be sorry,' I replied shoving him backwards.

Howard calmed us both down, and promised me we'd only be another ten minutes.

'Mr. Glover states that you were jealous of his friendship with your girlfriend.'

'That's absolute rubbish,' I said. 'What's there to be jealous of him about, he's not exactly Mister Wonderful is he?'

'Brian we're all men of the world,' said Watts. 'We know what it's like to feel jealous.'

'You're wasting your time,' I said, 'I can't help you. Now I want to go to bed, my ten minutes are up.'

Howard reluctantly agreed to end the interview, but promised to continue the next day. There was no question of me being released as they were going to make more enquiries in the morning.

It was almost two-thirty in the morning, by the time I got back to the cells. After nearly two hours of non-stop questioning, I was tired but confident I hadn't made a mistake. Although I had won the first round in the contest, I was still the wrong side of the cell door.

Breakfast and lunch went by before they returned to interview me again. As soon as I walked into the room I knew I was free. The tired, dejected look on the face of DC Watts told the story of a fruitless search for the truth.

'We understand your girlfriend made a complaint against Glover,' said DC Howard. 'There wasn't anything to support the complaint, so we didn't take any action.'

'That is none taken by us anyhow,' muttered Watts sarcastically.

'What's that supposed to mean,' I snapped.

'We're only looking at possible motives, and you do appear to have quite a lot,' said Howard. 'Several people on your estate swear their was an incident on Tuesday night, but are too afraid to say anymore.'

'Really, I am surprised,' I said.

'We've been looking at your file,' said Howard, 'you've been riding your luck for a long time. This isn't the first time people have been too scared to testify against you.'

'Malicious wounding, violent assaults,' said Watts reading down the list on my file. All of them appear to have been dropped for one reason or another. Well you're not going to get away with this one. We know you tried to kill him, we may not be able to prove it, but I'm sure we'll find something.'

They released me on bail pending further inquiries. I walked out of the station feeling confident and victorious. Geordie and Johnno had been released earlier, and they were waiting in the pub for me.

'I thought they were never gonna let you out,' said Geordie.

'Do you reckon anyone will talk Bri?' asked Johnno, looking worried.

'According to Watts and Howard, their pretty scared,' I said, 'so it's not likely.'

'You went a bit too far,' said Johnno,' he was always gonna talk.'

'It looks like I didn't go far enough,' I said, with regret. 'I should have finished him off when I had the chance.'

'That guy's got more lives than a cat,' said Geordie.

'As far as I'm concerned he's just used up his last one,' I said.

Later, I returned to the estate and saw many worried faces looking out of their windows. I stared back at them with a confident grin beaming all over my face.

A month later I returned to the police station to answer my bail. I was shocked when I was told that I was being charged with threatening to murder with intent.

'You thought you were going to get away with it, didn't you?' sneered DC Watts.

They took me to a special court hearing held in the station. To my surprise the magistrates allowed me bail, although there were certain conditions.

'That's wiped the smile off your face,' laughed Watts, as I walked passed him. 'You see there are still some people who can't be intimidated by you.'

I tried to ignore his comment but it was hard, as I knew he was right. I returned home and kept a low profile for a while. During the long wait for my trial Glover tried to provoke me into a fight. He had pushed Karen and Leoni to the ground in a local furniture auction. Karen reported it to the police, but once again they declined to take any action. When I heard about it I promised the police I'd get even with them. Shortly after this, Karen left me for good and took Leoni with her.

I blamed Glover for their departure, and it made me more intent on killing him. I paid someone to give him a kicking, but they bottled out at the last minute. I was stopped from any further attempts, when I was given the chance to have Leoni to stay at weekends.

Within a few weeks, her stays became longer until she lived with me for most of the time. The relationship between us grew very strong, as I became both mother and father. Finally my trial arrived, and reluctantly I took her back to Karen for the last time.

At court, before the trial started, we had a conference with our barrister. The prosecution had offered a deal, based on us pleading guilty to lesser charges.

'I strongly advise you to except their offer,' said our barrister. 'If you're found guilty you could get anything up to fourteen years.'

'What sort of a deal?' asked Johnno.

'You and Geordie must plead guilty to criminal damage,' he said. 'Which only means a slap on the wrist.'

'That sounds pretty good,' said Geordie.

The deal for me wasn't quite as attractive. They wanted me to plead guilty to GBH and criminal damage. The threat to murder with intent, would also be held on file as unproven.

'Let's take it,' said Johnno.

I wasn't very keen on the idea, but I didn't have much choice after Johnno and Geordie accepted it. We waited in the dock while our barrister informed the court of our change of plea. The jury was dismissed and then the Judge turned his attention towards us.

'I'll not waste any time on you,' he said sternly. 'You're a danger to the public, and therefore I'm removing you immediately. I'm remanding you in custody until a date is set for sentencing.'

'That was some slap on the wrists,' I said, to Johnno and Geordie as we went down the steps to the cells. We shared the rest of my bottle of valium, while we waited for the transport to take us to Horfield Prison.

Chapter Seven

INSIDE

We were coming to the end of our journey, our destination Horfield Prison. As we approached the junction leading to the entrance, I could see it's walls towering high above the other buildings. It immediately gave the appearance of an impregnable castle. Very quickly we arrived at the outer gates, and I began to wonder what was awaiting me on the other side. It had been almost ten years since my last spell in prison, and I wondered what might have changed.

That time at seventeen, I had been in Pucklechurch Detention Centre. It was when borstals were still in use. The regime had been a tough one, with it's severe discipline. Everything was done army style, bed packs had to be made daily. Blanket, sheet, blanket, sheet, with the pillow case in between. The mattress had to be standing up against the wall until after the inspection was over. The floor of your cell had to be washed and scrubbed along with the landings. All your personal kit had to be spotless, with your boots shiny enough to see your face in. Physical education was compulsory, and at the double. The screws bawling you out for the slightest wrong-doing. It certainly was a harsh and sometimes frightening environment to live in.

The loud banging noise of the prison gates closing behind us, brought me back to reality. The last view of the outside world was shut from our sight.

'I hope they hurry up and take us off this bus, so I can get these cuffs off,' I said to the guy manacled to me.

'I'm not in any hurry,' he said nervously.

Our escort arrived and quickly took us to the reception area. On the way we passed through the inner perimeter gate. This was situated within a twenty foot high fence which ran round the inside of the wall. At reception we were made welcome. 'Strip off,' came a loud voice from behind the desk. We threw our own clothes into a bag, which then disappeared out of sight. Quickly we were ushered through the showers, and then brought in front of the doctor. It was all a bit like being in a cattle market.

The doctor was looking at my empty bottle of valium. 'What are these for?' he asked.

'I've been on valium for several years,' I said, 'and I have to take them daily.'

'You won't be getting any of them in here,' he said. 'We are not in the habit of supplying drugs.'

'I've a legal prescription,' I said protesting.

'Your prescription doesn't carry any weight in here,' he said, unmoved.

'But what am I going to do?' I asked concerned.

'Next,' was all I got as he disregarded my plea. I left and put on my clothes, knowing my argument was futile.

Surprisingly the prison issue clothes weren't too bad. The shirts were really quite smart, and the rest of the gear was passable. The only exception was the underpants which hung halfway down your legs. Still it didn't matter as I hadn't any plans for a night on the town. On the way over to the main part of the prison we picked up the rest of our belongings. This didn't consist of much, shaving brush, tooth powder and a bar of white windsor soap.

We entered A Wing, which was going to be my new home for a while. It was half-past seven in the evening as we came to the cell door. There was quite a lot of activity going on, as some of the inmates were watching television. I was shown a card with my details on, which was placed on the door. My new title, Name Russ; Number T68011. The cell was very small, about eight feet by twelve, with a window too high to see out. It was originally designed for one person, but now with terrible overcrowding, four men shared it. There were two sets of bunk beds, a table, chairs, a solitary sanitation bucket and a jug and bowl for washing.

All four of us had come in that night, so we started out equal. There were some other occupants, who were there first, the spiders, and cockroaches. Who knows what they thought of us. Eight o'clock came and we were locked up for the night.

Nothing much was said, as we all lay back on our bunks with our own thoughts. For me, my main concern was how I was going to cope without my valium. The only good thing was that I had reduced my intake considerably to one every couple of days. Maybe I would be able to get hold of something to take its place later. I blocked out all thoughts of Leoni, as I wasn't likely to see her for a while. However I was concerned about my dog, because he was locked in the flat, expecting me to come home. I soon fell asleep, and thought no more about him.

The rattle of keys and the clanging of doors woke me up the next morning. As I cleared my eyes I realised I hadn't been dreaming, but I was really inside. The heavy footsteps arrived outside our door, the lock turned and the door flew open. 'Slop out,' came the shout from our jailer.

'What no good morning?' joked one of my cellmates. With that we trooped out, and joined the long queue for the sluice room. Slopping out was a particulary horrible job, which took place several times a day. The process was to tip out your toilet receptacle and rinse it out.

After washing and shaving we lined up for breakfast. With my tray I approached the hot-plate, 'egg, bacon, sausage or beans,' said the inmate serving.

'A bit of everything please,' I said.

'No, only one choice,' he said with a laugh.

I took an egg, and sampled some of the notorious porridge.

'You're not going to eat that are you?' said my cellmate, 'it's made of pig oats, for animals.'

'I'll try anything once,' I said.

'It makes really good paste for sticking pictures on the wall,' he said.

Sure enough, he was right, as I gave it a try. I wondered what it must be doing to the inside of my stomach. As breakfast came and went, so did dinner, and tea, and so the cycle went on.

As I was awaiting sentence, I wasn't allowed to have a job, so I remained banged up twenty-three hours a day. For the other hour, we had exercise on the yard, but sometimes this was cancelled if the weather was bad. On exercise some people were busy trying to scrounge a smoke, including myself. Times were hard, esecially as I wasn't working. Life on the dole meant you only got £1.37 for all luxuries. Most people would walk round for a bit, then sit down with a group they felt comfortable with.

There was one guy in particular who walked round the yard for the whole hour. He would come out, strip off to the waist like an athlete and walk round very briskly. One lap consisted of about one hundred metres, and he would easily do fifty or sixty laps.

Back on the wing we waited eagerly for our turn to watch television. On A Wing there were four landings so this meant we only got to watch it every fourth night. The other nights were rotated with showers and kit change. Just as I had got used to the cell I was in, they moved us to another wing, where we were all split up. It was quite a good laugh in my new cell. The pranks that we got up to, were more like that of a boarding school than a nick. Nobody knew who the victim would be, as we played tricks on each other at the same time. French sheets in the bed was a good one, where you would fold the bottom sheet in two and tuck it in. The person would try to get into bed, but could only manage to get their feet in.

We all collected insects, and made them our pets. You might find yourself in bed with Harry the spider, or Colin the cockroach. The bed linen was supposed to have been fire-proof, so one night in our cell we put it to the test. Sid always slept fully clothed in bed, and very rarely bothered to wash. By the sink, was a can of boot resin, like a kind of oil. We poured it over the bottom of his bed and his boots. To our amazement it caught fire when we lit it. Sid just laughed, 'I'm not getting up, I'd rather burn alive, than get out of bed.'

'Call the fire-brigade,' came a shout.

'Here I come,' I said, carrying a bucket of water, 'and there it goes,' throwing the water on the fire and Sid.

All these games helped us to focus on something other than our own personal situations. However I was still pretty bored, so I pleaded with the senior officer on my wing to give me a job. Fortunately for me there was a vacancy that day among the cleaners, so he let me have it. I was on the move once again, this time on the second floor where the cleaners had their own landing. I only spent one day at the job before I was summoned back to court.

Without any notice they took me off to reception to board the coach. I had waited months to be sentenced, but apparently the judge had been ill. It was strange to be in my own clothes and going out the gate, only I did wonder how long it was for.

My appearance in the dock was a brief one. There had been a lot of discussion between counsel and the judge about what was best to do. Before he passed sentence he gave me a severe tongue lashing.

'In my view you are a particularly dangerous individual, who shows no thought to anyone in society,' he said. 'If you hadn't been stopped, I've no doubt that it would've resulted in a loss of life.' He was certainly working himself up to something as he continued. 'I am sending you to prison for one year, with a recommendation for the other offences to be taken into account.'

I started to fidget in my seat, wondering when he might stop. 'Furthermore I order that the charge of threatening to murder with intent be laid on file, then should you appear in court again it will be activated immediately.'

The all too familiar words of 'take them down' was given, and we were quickly on our way down the steps, to the cells. We had been first on that morning, so there had been no time for worrying. The trouble was that we had the rest of the day waiting for everybody else. There was nothing to do here, except think about your sentence.

The judge had put a lot of effort into trying to get his message across to me, but I wasn't impressed. 'Did he really think I was bothered by his idle threats?' I thought. No matter what anyone says, nothing was going to stop me having my revenge one day. After a long wait, we were finally on our way back to Horfield. The return trip didn't take as long as this morning's did. I think the screws were in a hurry to get home. The judge must have been in a bad mood, because the coach was almost full.

My day trip out came to an end as we drove into the prison courtyard. Fortunately I didn't have to wait too long to be processed, and I was allowed to go back on the wing. On my return, I had to go into the office to find out my location. The Senior Officer was standing at the desk with a smile on his face.

'Same cell as this morning for you,' he said. 'I've kept your job open, as I thought you would be back tonight.'

I was pleased to have retained my job, and my cell, it would have been a pain to start afresh. On the landing a lot of the guys were waiting to welcome me back.

'How did it go?' said Tosh, 'good result was it?'

'Depends how you look at it,' I replied. 'Let's put it this way, I won't be expecting Father Christmas this year.'

'Couldn't you stay away?' said our landing screw as he came to lock up.

'I didn't want you and the boys to get lonely,' I said. He was a fairly decent bloke for a screw, you could have a laugh with him.

Life became far easier on the cleaners, as there were a number of perks to the job. On my job, we had to work seven days a week, so as a result we were unlocked all the time except meal times and at night.

Every wing had it's own kitchen servery area, where the food came over on trolleys. We had to help dish up, and afterwards wash up all the trays and serving dishes. We would wash two hundred trays each mealtime, and as one tray had three compartments, it was equal to washing six hundred plates. Although the food wasn't great, I could take what I wanted. When I served the food, I looked after my mates and they looked after me. Now my lifestyle had improved, I set about creating some wealth for myself. All the cleaners were paid on Sunday's, another privilege. This was great as the weekends were long, and without a smoke they were even longer.

As I strolled onto the exercise yard, I was swamped by several inmates. 'Can you spare us a smoke mate?' they cried.

'Here's one between you,' I said, feeling generous.

Some of the guy's I had originally come in with came over. 'Bri sell us some snout,' said John, 'we haven't got a smoke in the whole of our cell.'

'As it's you,' I said, 'I'll let you have it cheap, half-ounce now for three-quarters tomorrow.'

'Sound's fair enough,' he said. A deal was made, and my career in the market place began.

I saved myself enough tobacco for that day, and traded the rest, two for one. In prison the exchange rate was a lot higher than outside, generally there was 100% mark up on all goods. The next day, during tea, I was paid off by those who owed me. I was feeling quite pleased with myself as I had made a profit of three-quarters of an ounce. There were several guys throughout the prison who traded regular, but there were plenty of customers to be had. It could be a risky business at times, because all such trading was strictly illegal. Usually you only lent to those who could afford to pay you back, but occasionly there were bad debts. These had to be taken care of quickly and at times violently. A failure to do so, could soon lead to you going broke.

One of my cellmates was the cleaner in the visits room, where every day he collected all the left over fag stubs. We came to an arrangement where I paid him half an ounce of good tobacco for half of all his dog-ends for the whole week. Although these were butts, most of them were only half smoked, leaving a fair amount. Throughout the dinner-time bang up, we would take the tobacco out of the butts, and divide it up. Most days my share was over half an ounce, which when sold, would show me a healthy profit.

I did business with another inmate, who worked in the officers mess. He supplied me with a jar of coffee, and a bag of sugar, which cost half an ounce. To make good coffee, you've got to have milk, which I got from the guys in the kitchen. As I came down into the TV room, I heard John say, 'Look out here comes The Baron.'

'What have you got for us tonight then Bri,' he said grinning.

'I'm afraid I've only got coffee,' I said, 'but it's made with real milk.'

'Has it got sugar?' he said.

'No, sugar's extra,' I said, laughing.

'Your rates are getting a bit steep Baron,' said John, looking worried.

'I'm only kidding,' I said. 'Of course it's got sugar in it, I'm not completely heartless.'

We made a deal, three mugs of coffee, for a Mars bar and a packet of biscuits. It might have seemed tough amongst mates, but it was the survival of the fittest in here.

On the prison stock exchange, drugs had the most value. Tobacco was next with money third, and gold coming last. My cellmates all came from Bristol so they had regular visits, when drugs were smuggled in. Most guys were looking to score, so it was fairly easy to trade. Enough was kept for our own use, and the rest was sold throughout the wings.

When things needed to be delivered the insole of your shoe was a good hiding place. Many times I walked the landings with my shoes filled with contraband of one sort or another. Cash, tobacco and drugs exchanged hands very quickly, because nobody enjoyed holding it for long. To be caught with a stash of drugs or money meant serious trouble. There were all kinds of drugs on offer, from cannabis to heroin. From Friday to Sunday, we'd be so smashed, on LSD and cannabis, that we struggled to get out of bed.

On our landing at weekends, you could get stoned just by standing near our door. Most of the screws knew it was going on, they had to be pretty green if they didn't know. There were cell searches, but usually we were one step ahead of them, knowing when they were likely to happen.

However one Friday evening by accident, we came unstuck. It was after tea and there was no association for the prison that night because of kit change. We thought it would be safe to have a smoke, so we made ourselves a bucket bong. This was a plastic bottle with the bottom cut off, placed in a bucket of water. A piece of gauze was inside a funnel with the lighted drug and tobacco mixture. The bottle was submerged up to it's neck until it was full of smoke. Then the funnel was taken out, and you put your mouth over the top, inhaling as the bottle surfaced. A full bottle was hard to take in one go, as it was very potent this way.

We urged each other on as we took it in turns, to see who could master it. We all had two full bottles each, out of the batch made up. The bucket was on the table right next to my bed. After taking my turn I was so stoned I found it almost impossible to reach it. As this was going on, unknown to us the screws were having a head count, as one guy was late returning from home leave. Unexpectedly they arrived at our door and looked through the spy hole, just as the bong was being dismantled. Panic and chaos broke out in the cell as we desperately tried to lose the evidence out the window. The sound of boots running arrived and the door crashed open.

'Right everybody out,' shouted the leading screw.

'What's wrong guv?' came an innocent voice.

'You know what we're after,' he said impatiently.

We were quickly ushered outside, and made to stand against the wall. As we were all stoned, it was difficult to control ourselves. Taffy had been the only one they saw at the table, so he was called in.

'Come on, tell us where you've hidden it,' we heard them ask. 'Hid what?' said Taffy, 'I don't know what you're talking about.' Taffy came back out, and the search continued. We all looked at Taffy for a sign, he shook his head and whispered, 'they've got nothing.'

We waited anxiously, hoping that he was right. We all knew the consequences of being found out. Possession of drugs, was a far more serious offence in prison than outside, and was dealt with severely. It always meant extra bird through loss of remission, but it could mean an outside court, with another sentence.

After half an hour they came out and to our relief they were empty handed. 'Get that mess in there cleaned up,' they said angrily, walking off.

We went back into our cell which was now looking like a rubbish tip. They had emptied the contents of our lockers out on the floor. Sugar, coffee and milk powder was now mixed with tobacco and ash. In spite of their efforts, we managed to save most of it.

'They sure know how to demolish a persons home,' said Tosh sadly.

'Never mind, it's a small price to pay,' I said. 'The look on their faces when they left, was well worth it.'

We had won the first round in the game of chance, but another time we might not be so lucky.

Chapter Eight

PARDONED

Looking at the daily paper, I quickly worked out how long I had left inside. There was exactly one hundred days to go before I could unlock my own door.

It was the first time I'd really given serious thought about being released. I was looking forward to seeing my daughter Leoni again, as I'd missed her terribly. However I wasn't in a rush to get back to Devizes. The only thing waiting for me there was a hostile neighbourhood and a man who I wanted dead.

Apart from seeing Leoni, getting Glover was the only other thing that had kept me going through my sentence. I discussed the possibility of a contract killing on him with two other inmates. But the desire to kill him myself made me change my mind. Since then I had worked out a way of killing him, without getting caught. This meant leaving him alone for over a year, but I could wait.

'Hey Bri, there's a transfer to Erlestoke Prison next week,' said Sid walking into my cell. 'I'm going, you ought to try and get on it as well.'

Erlestoke prison was only six miles from Devizes. It was a semi-open nick, which meant it only had a fence for a perimeter. I'd only received one visit since being inside, and that was when I was on remand. 'Maybe if I go there, I might get a visit,' I thought.

I went to see the Senior Officer, and asked if he'd consider me for the transfer. He was quite sympathetic towards me, and promised to look into it. Later that day he called me back into the office. It was bad news, as the security staff had refused to let me go. 'I'm sorry, you're going to Dartmoor instead,' he said. 'You're still classed as a high risk, so you can't go to a semi-open nick.'

I wasn't too bothered about being turned down for Erlestoke. I had managed to get by without visits up to now, so a few more months wouldn't hurt.

The night before the transfer to Erlestoke Prison, the Senior Officer called me into his office again.

'You're going to Erlestoke in the morning transfer after all,' he said.

'How come?' I asked feeling stunned.

'Don't ask me,' he said. 'Your name's on the list, how it got there I've no idea.'

I wasn't going to argue about it. If they had made a mistake that was their tough luck.

Early the next morning all those for transfer and court arrived at reception. Within an hour we were boarding a coach to take us to Erlestoke. As we drove away from Horfield, I looked back for the last time at what had been my home. I wondered how long it might be, before I saw it again.

For security reasons the coaches used for transferring prisoners always travelled by the same route. The Erlestoke coach normally went through Bath and Westbury, but we found ourselves on our way to Chippenham. This meant we would have to go through Devizes to get to Erlestoke.

As we approached the edge of Devizes, I began to wonder if I would see anyone I knew. To my horror I caught a glimpse of Glover going into one of the pubs. My heart started beating faster and my knuckles turned white, as I clenched my fists. The thought of him having a beer and enjoying himself, made me want to jump off the coach and throttle him.

Thankfully before I had time to consider it further, we had left Devizes behind.

Within fifteen minutes we were entering the grounds of Erlestoke Prison. My first impression of it reminded me of a P.O.W camp, from out an old war film. Fortunately the accommodation blocks, were a lot better. The all too familiar reception ritual was over quickly, and we were soon swallowed up in the system.

The atmosphere on the wing was totally dead, where Horfield Prison was a hive of activity. Every inmate had his own cell, so there was a lot more privacy. Bang up only occurred at night and after meals, so there was a lot more freedom also.

I was given a job working on the maintenance of the prison grounds. After a couple of days I was allowed to drive one of the tractors, and operate the machinery. Every morning I was let through the gate to the sports field to mow and roll the grass. The field was situated on the far side of the prison, overlooking Devizes.

After being let through, I remained there unsupervised until lunchtime. Once I was alone, there was only a single fence between me and freedom. Day after day I stood staring through the fence towards Devizes, thinking of Glover and revenge. Since my arrival I had thought of nothing else. My thoughts were interrupted when a screw shouted to me that I had a probation visit.

'What do you want?' I said, aggressively at the probation officer as I walked in.

He introduced himself and told me he was acting on behalf of the police and local council.

'The authorities are concerned about what might happen when you're released,' he said.

44

'So they should be,' I said.

'All parties concerned, are willing to come together to try and find a solution to this problem. One thing that has been suggested, is for you to move to another area.'

My plan to get Glover included me moving away, but now I was being told to, I wasn't so keen.

'I'm not moving out for anyone,' I snapped.

'Couldn't you at least give it a try, everyone else is. The police wish to avoid any further conflict with you.'

'Oh do they,' I said, beginning to boil over. 'Well that's too bad because I've not finished with them yet. They lost any chance of peace, when they declared war on me.

'Why's that?' he asked.

'Look I don't want to talk anymore,' I said getting up to go.

'But I haven't finished yet,' he said.

'Just clear off,' I said angrily. 'I don't need this aggravation, I'll sort out my problems my own way.' I walked out, leaving him sitting there open mouthed.

The visit had got me so wound up, that by teatime I couldn't eat my food. I sat on the bed and tried to relax, but it was no good my anger was boiling over. Trying to hide my feelings for Glover during the visit was too much for me. I desperately wanted to tell the probation officer what I had planned for Glover, but I knew I couldn't.

In the evening during association I tried to buy some drugs, but sadly there was none to be had at any price. Erlestoke was useless for drugs, as hardly anyone could smuggle then in. I longed to be back in Horfield where drugs were easily available.

Time for bang up came and I returned to my cell still feeling agitated. As the screws were locking up, one of them gave me a letter which had been mislaid. It was such a shock seeing my name on an envelope that I could only stare at it at first. The last letter I'd received was from my solicitor just after I'd been sentenced. Although I wrote regularly to my family, I never received any in return.

It was even more of a shock to find it was from Karen. Any pleasure I may have had from receiving the letter, turned to misery as I read it through.

'I just want you to know that I am moving. Since you've been in Prison Leoni and I have grown closer. My fiance is getting Posted abroad next month, and Leoni and I are going with him.

'You're not the type of person I want her father to be. She was only one year old, when you went inside, so she won't remember you. It's for the best that you never see her again.

'In fact, as far as I'm concerned she'll never know that you

45

existed. As soon as we're married, she'll be brought up to think that my fiance is her dad.

'PS It's not worth trying to find out where we've gone as the army never gives out information.'

I read it through again hoping I'd made a mistake. Sadly, there wasn't anything wrong with my eyesight. 'Why Me?' I cried, shaking my fist. I sat down on the floor, and took out the tiny photograph of my daughter Leoni. As I looked at it, I started to remember the last time we spent together.

It was just after her first birthday, when she was struck down with a mysterious virus and went to hospital. Inside the children's ward I stayed by her bedside, helping to nurse her. For three days and nights I waited anxiously for her to recover. I wanted to take her place, to carry her pain and stop her tears. If I left the room for anything she would cry out for me.

'I would give anything to hear her call out to me once more,' I said, as I stopped dreaming. I wished it were possible to stay inside my dream with her forever, but sadly reality was always there.

Throughout my sentence, I always believed that one day I would see Leoni again. Now the only person in the world who mattered to me, was gone forever.

'Not much to show for nearly thirty years of pain,' I said, feeling choked up.

In one second the whole of my life had been wiped out, leaving nothing but an empty shell. Even now when my misery was complete, I couldn't cry. I wanted to, but I didn't know how. The tears were there, but they couldn't find a way out. There didn't seem any point in carrying on living any longer, as I was only suffering. I had decided to end my life there and then, when suddenly a picture of Glover's face stopped me.

'How could I kill him if I was dead,' I thought.

Soon Glover became the target for all my pain and grief. As far as I was concerned, he was to blame for all my tragedies. I gave myself a last minute reprieve and promised to see Glover die first. I was being released on New Years Eve, so I swore an oath to myself that Glover and I would both die on January the first.

I had sentenced Glover to death a long time ago, all I would be doing was bring his execution forward. It was strange that I should want to die with the person I hated the most. All my life I wanted to be somebody, now I would be, as no one would forget my end. I wasn't afraid to die, because for me death meant freedom from my pain.

I got up and looked out of the window, and saw it was already getting light. Soon the screws would be coming round to unlock our cells. While I waited for them to come I began to realise what it must be like to be on death row. For me these last days before my release was my death row. Although it was my choice to kill and be killed, there was nothing I could do to stop it.

Over the next two days I began to withdraw from everyone as my obsession with death grew. The only person I spoke to was the prison chaplain. I had asked him to visit me because I wanted to tell someone why I was going to kill.

The chaplain was a smallish man of about fifty, with a little grey beard. When I first arrived at Erlestoke, he arranged for me to have a phone call to my parents. Unfortunately the conversation I had with them was unpleasant. By the time he arrived I wasn't in the mood to talk anymore, but he wasn't put off.

'Are you still upset about your family?' he asked.

'I haven't got a family,' I said miserably. 'In fact I've been robbed of the only family I've ever had.'

I told him as much as I wanted him to know, without going into any details. He agreed that everything I told him was in confidence.

'You know God can help, if you let him,' he said.

'There is no God,' I said, sharply, 'at least not for the likes of me.'

'Jesus loves everyone, including you,' he said softly.

'I'm an evil person,' I said, 'I think I must be an exception.'

'There are no exceptions,' he said. 'Jesus accepts us, just the way we are.'

He wrote a prayer in the back of a Bible and left it for me on my table. He told me I might find it comforting. Before he left, he prayed for me to find peace. Within minutes of him leaving, the screws came and locked me up for the night.

I sat for several hours with my head in my hands, trying to shut out the whole world. It was an impossible task, as the faces of Leoni and Glover kept flashing back and forth. This only succeeded in winding me up further, making my muscles go into a spasm, causing immense pain. I lifted my head, only to find myself facing the bible which the chaplain had left.

I wondered what he had written in the back of it, and started to reach out to pick it up.

'No don't bother, it's only rubbish,' I said, withdrawing my hand again.

It seemed to be staring up at me from the table, making me even more curious. Finally after thirty minutes of looking at nothing else I picked it up. Quickly I turned to the back of the book, to where the chaplain had written. I read aloud :

47

'Lord Jesus Christ, Son of God, have mercy on me a sinner. Thank you for dying on the cross in my place, and coming back to life again.

Please forgive me all my sins, as I am truly sorry for all that I have done wrong. Please come into my life, and be my Lord and Saviour now and always. Fill me with your Holy Spirit, and make me new.
Amen

I read it through several times, trying to understand what it meant. To begin with it was like struggling with a foreign menu.

'A sinner I could understand,' I thought, 'but forgiveness, Saviour and the Holy Spirit was something else.' I looked upwards, wondering if there was anything there, but all I could see was the grey concrete ceiling.

'Look here God,' I said, beginning to talk to the ceiling. 'I don't think you exist, but if you do, stay out of my life. I'm going to kill that creep Glover and myself, and nobody can stop me.'

If I couldn't stop myself, I didn't see how anybody else could. I was on a roller coaster ride to death, and it didn't have any brakes. I continued to talk to the ceiling, as I had nothing else better to do.

'If you are a God, where have you been all the times I needed help?' I asked sarcastically.

Quite suddenly my hard attitude softened, and I found myself on my knees. In a last desperate attempt to stop the destruction I decided to give God a chance.

'It's me again God,' I said. 'I'd like to give you a try, but the problem is, I don't believe in you. I'd like to, but I can't believe in something I can't see.'

I began to pray the prayer which the chaplain had written in the Bible earlier. With all my heart I prayed it over and over again.

'Please Jesus help me believe in You,' I begged. 'I haven't bowed to anyone, but if you're real, I'll bow to you.'

For twenty minutes I tried desperately to get through the concrete to God. After a while I began to despair, when I realised I was still alone. I got up from the floor and laid on the bed, and made my final appeal.

'Jesus, please don't reject me,' I cried. 'If you want me, I want you, so please, please come and save me now.'

For a while everything was still, then slowly my icy cell started to feel warm. Immediately after, something that resembled a glowing light filled my cell. As it did I felt instant relief from all the pain and stress in my body.

I took a deep breath as the light entered my body. It appeared to cut it's way through my stomach, like a surgeon with a knife. All my strength appeared to drain out of me, as if I were about to die. I felt my flesh pull as all the hatred was torn out by it's roots. With my strength all gone and feeling completely empty, I was filled back up again by a fresh wave of energy. It was like I'd been plugged into an electric socket without getting a shock.

For the first time in my life, I felt safe and secure. I knew for sure that Jesus was different than other people. He accepted me just as the chaplain told me he would. As the night passed the light remained, speaking to me, yet not uttering any words.

'Was I still in the cell,' I thought, as I looked around. It appeared I was, yet I no longer felt like a prisoner. I felt like a totally new person.

How long this vision lasted I couldn't tell. It all seem to happen in seconds yet it was now morning. I could hear the screws coming down the landing and beginning to unlock the cells. I couldn't remember going to sleep or waking up, just sitting peacefully on my bed.

'Come on wakey wakey,' went the shout from the screw as he opened my door.

'Good morning,' I said, cheerfully.

'I'm sorry, did I hear you right?' he asked in amazement. He was startled by my comment because my attitude was always hostile.

'You sure did mate,' I replied, as I walked up to the toilets to slop out. Instead of the usual heaviness in my step, it now felt like I was walking on top of the air.

On my return from the toilets, I saw the screw coming out of my cell. He seemed confused and troubled as he looked me up and down. When I asked him what was wrong he grunted something about my appearance being different.

After breakfast I read the prayer in the bible again, and recalled the nights events. I was so excited about what had happened to me, that I wanted to tell the whole world.

Chapter Nine

A FRESH START

It was tea-time before I got the opportunity to tell someone about what I'd experienced the night before. The guy in the cell next to me, was the first person I told. He hadn't been with us very long, so I didn't know much about him.

'Hi, I'm Brian,' I said poking my head round his cell door.

'My names Derek,' he said inviting me in. 'I tried speaking to you the other day,' he said, 'but you didn't seem to be very happy.'

'Sorry about that,' I said. 'I used to be an ignorant pig, but that's all over now.'

'Why's that?' he asked.

I told him about my vision of Jesus Christ, and how a light entered my body.

'You don't believe me do you?' I said. 'Well I don't blame you really, it does sound a bit bizarre.'

'No I believe you,' said Derek. 'I've heard about things like that happening before.'

We spent the evening talking about our lives, and how we had ended up in prison.

Derek was a quiet and timid character of about fifty. This was his first time in prison, and he was finding it tough. He had been given six months for drinking and driving on his first offence.

'I've never been in any trouble before,' he said, 'not even for a parking ticket.'

'That sounds a bit harsh,' I said sympathetically.

He'd been the innocent party in an accident, but because he failed the breathalyser he got the blame.

'Both me and the other driver got injured,' he said, showing me his crippled foot.

'I only had two pints,' he said, 'still I've learnt my lesson.'

'It must be quite tough on your family?' I asked.

'I haven't seen my wife since I was sentenced a month ago,' he said sadly. 'I don't expect to either, now I've moved here.'

He and his wife worked on a country estate. There wasn't any public transport, and his wife couldn't drive.

'Can't somebody else bring her,' I said, trying help.

'No, I'm a game-keeper or at least I used to be,' he said. 'We don't have many neighbours, and most of our friends live too far away.'

Derek and his wife had been married for thirty years and this was the first time they'd ever been apart.

'I'll pray for you tonight Derek,' I said.

'Do you think it will do any good?' he asked.

'If he helped a person like me, I'm sure he'll help you,' I said.

Before I got into bed that night, I prayed for poor old Derek. I really felt sorry for him, as I knew what it was like to have no visitors.

The next day, I continued to ask Jesus to comfort Derek, and to let him hear from his wife.

Later that day after work, I was on my way to the showers, when Derek shouted to me.

'Come in my cell a minute,' he said grinning, 'I've got some great news to tell you.'

'You look like you've won the pools mate,' I said.

'Much better than that,' he said, 'I've had a visit from my wife.'

'That's great news,' I said happily.'

'It must have been your prayers that made a difference,' he said, 'as it was a miracle.'

An old friend of Derek's wife turned up at their house unexpectedly. They hadn't seen her for over six years, so she had no idea that he was in prison.

'They just jumped in her car and came straight over,' he said. 'Now is there anything I can do for you Brian?'

'Would you go to church with me over Christmas?' I asked. 'I've never been before, so you'd be doing me a favour.'

'Yes, alright,' he said. 'I haven't been for a while, although we used to go every week.'

From then on Derek and I prayed together every night, and we became very good friends.

A couple of nights later I was listening to the radio, when a newsflash came on. It was news of a terrible tragedy that had taken place near the Phillipines. A boat load of people, mainly women and children had sunk a few miles off the coast. There were no survivors, and the rescue services were giving up the search.

I switched off the radio and knelt on the floor to pray. My eyes began to fill up with tears as I pictured the wreckage. I wanted to go and save the children, but that was not possible. I thought of all the children who had drowned, and how frightened they must have been. The times I had felt sorry for myself over my own tragedies made me feel ashamed. With tears in my eyes, I prayed that God would somehow save some of them.

'Lord, even if you save one,' I cried, 'I'll know you did it for me. I returned to bed, feeling a little better now that I had done something to help. It was a strange experience for me, to feel pain and sorrow for another human being.

Early the next morning, I switched on the radio just as the news came on. The reporter was getting excited as he told listeners of a great miracle. At least one child from the boat disaster in the Phillipines, had been found alive. The report stated that the child appeared from nowhere.

'Oh thank you Lord,' I shouted, punching the air with excitement. Experiencing the miracles of God was more thrilling than all the drugs and drink I'd taken. It was also reassuring to know that God was still with me, because in a few days I would be free.

I had mixed feelings about getting out. In prison I felt safe and confident, but outside the world seemed cold and unfriendly. Once outside the gates, the fear of forgetting Jesus, and him forgetting me worried me. The distractions and hostilities that were waiting for me outside, could make me forget.

'Lord, will you remember me when I'm free?' I asked.

To help me remember him, I wrote a letter and posted it to my home address. It contained the details of my conversion, and all the answered prayers I'd had.

Before I could enjoy my release, I had to get through Christmas. In prison this was a gloomy prospect, for screw and con alike.

Christmas day arrived bringing sadness and misery, instead of presents and joy. The atmosphere changed from it's normal relaxed attitude, to one of immense tension. It was very quiet as everyone went about the usual morning routine of slopping out. A special effort was made by all, not to say anything to upset anyone. Wishing each other a merry Christmas was especially off limits.

Most of the inmates had their heads down so as not to show their faces. It was clear that nearly everyone was suffering from depression. The call for church came shortly after breakfast for those who wanted to go.

I had heard this call many times before, but this was the first time I was answering it. I walked up to the wing gate, to be let through, only to be met by our landing officer.

'Where do you think you're going?' he said questioningly.

'Church sir,' I said smartly.

'You've never been to church before,' he said suspiciously.

'There's always a first time for everything,' I said, rather cheekily.

'I smell a rat,' he said, letting me through the gate. 'You're up to something, I'm sure of it.'

'I'm going to say some prayers,' I said truthfully. 'I'll say one for you while I'm there.'

'I know you're trying to work your ticket for parole,' he said confidently.

'Wrong again sir, I'm afraid,' I said, walking off. 'I'm getting out on Thursday so I don't need it.'

I entered the chapel feeling anxious, as I didn't know what to expect.

My fears subsided when I saw the chaplain, and explained about my encounter in the cell. He was pleased, and invited me to share in Communion. There was only a handful of people in church, and three of them were staff. However the service was good, and the attitude of the others towards me was one of friendship.

Going to church and taking Communion, had been the high point of the day. Unfortunately the rest of the Christmas festivities didn't compare too well with it.

For our lunch we had processed turkey, which was awful. Christmas pudding was served for lunch and tea, except for tea it had icing on it. To our relief Christmas day came to an end.

The next couple of days went by fairly quickly, leaving me with my last night banged up. It was hard to get to sleep, because I couldn't stop thinking of freedom in the morning. While I lay there, I remembered the faces of the inmates on Christmas day.

I prayed that they might soon be with their families and loved ones.

As I prayed, the face of my daughter Leoni appeared in my mind. I'd hardly had time to think about her since my conversion. I knew that I would probably never see her again, so I just asked the Lord to take care of her.

I wiped away a tear that had formed in my eye, as I prayed for her to be safe. 'You'll be able to look after her better than I could Lord,' I said, turning over to go to sleep.

Morning quickly came round, and I left my cell for the last time. I said goodbye to Derek and gave him all my belongings.

'Aren't you having any breakfast Russ?' asked our landing officer.

'No fear, I don't want to get the guts-ache now.' I said laughing. Soon I was on my way to the reception, and changing back into my own clothes. Once I was dressed, it was only a matter of minutes before I was walking through the gates to freedom.

The journey from the Prison to Devizes, was a short one, so I was outside my parents house by nine o'clock. In spite of feeling let down by them, we had managed to resolve our differences over the telephone. They had been looking after my dog, Luke, while I was in prison. Luke didn't recognise me at first, but by the time he'd sniffed me, his memory returned. He started jumping up and licking me.

'He's remembered your smell,' said my youngest brother Philip.

'I must have ponged a bit then,' I said with a laugh. It was really nice to receive such a friendly welcome, even if it was only from a dog!

My parents and I agreed to make a fresh start. They invited me to stay at their house, while I sorted out my affairs. I wasn't in a hurry to go home, but a couple of days at their house was enough for me.

As I returned to the housing estate where I lived, it became obvious I wasn't getting a hero's welcome. Curtains were being drawn and the finger pointing was beginning. I wasn't keen on having a showdown with the neighbours, so I quickly got to my flat. It was a strange thing for me to be the one who was doing the hiding, but now I felt I had more to fear from them.

Waiting for me inside was a large amount of post. There on the top of the pile, was the one I had sent to myself from prison. After reading it through I put it on the mantlepiece as a reminder of where I'd been.

Over the next few days I stayed indoors, and kept a low profile. It was easier than facing the neighbours hostility. Glover still lived next door to me, although I hadn't seen him. I was uncertain what my reaction would be if I saw him, so I decided not to look at him.

After a week of living indoors I thought it was time I made an appearance in the town. I met Geordie and Johnno in the pub for a drink, and told them that I was following Jesus. They just laughed and told me not to be so silly.

When we separated, I went into the police station to sort out my differences with them. During my trial I had made it known that I was going to kill them.

'What do you want?' asked Howard nervously. 'We don't want any trouble.'

'No trouble,' I said, holding out my hand in a friendly gesture. 'I've come to apologise for the threats I made towards you.'

'Pardon,' said Watts shocked.

I repeated my apology, and told them about my experience of Christ. They stared at me with their mouths open, unable to speak. Whether it was disbelief or shock I couldn't say. I walked out and returned to my flat.

My brother Philip was waiting for me when I got back. He had a message from Karen, asking me to phone her. At first I thought it was a practical joke but when I phoned, I found it wasn't.

Her relationship with her fiance had ended, and she was no longer moving away. We arranged to meet the next day, so I could see Leoni. The idea of seeing her again, was something I had only dreamt of, but tomorrow my dream would come true.

Chapter Ten

UPS AND DOWNS

Tomorrow soon became today, as I arrived at Karen's parents house to see Leoni. It was a relief to find Karen's family being so nice towards me, especially after being in prison.

Leoni was sat in the living room, dressed in her best clothes. At first she was shy, but after some persuasion, she began to accept me. The change in her was quite startling, because now she was walking and talking. Although the visit was short it was positive, because Karen agreed to let me visit on a regular basis.

Over the next few weeks the relationship between the three of us continued to grow. Broken fences began to be mended between Karen and I, as the new me began to win her over. For Leoni's sake we agreed to make a fresh start together. We set a date for when they would return to live with me at the flat.

As I had been very busy sorting things out, I hadn't got round to going to church. Before Karen and Leoni returned I tried to put that right. In prison the few of us who followed Jesus were as one. Sadly outside I found that there were so many differences, I wasn't sure where to look.

There were a few people who I knew were Christians, so I decided to seek their support. I spoke to them about my conversion, and hoped that I might be accepted. Unfortunately I felt rejected, when my story appeared not to be believed. After that experience I decided to worship God alone rather than try any of the churches. At first I managed quite well on my own. I prayed and read the bible twice a day, but after Karen and Leoni returned to live, it got less.

I got a job working on an airbase for a building firm. God must have been helping me, because I was cleared through their security. It was the best job I'd ever had in my life. With a few wage packets in my pocket I was able to buy myself a van.

Back at the flat, my relationship with Karen began to deteroriate. She'd only been back a month before she was spending every weekend at her parents home. Karen assured me that it was only a temporary arrangement, while she sorted something out. I thought it was a bit odd, but I had no reason to doubt her.

On her next visit to her parents, she didn't return as normal, so I drove over to find out why. When I arrived she became angry and abusive towards me.

'What do you want?' said Karen sharply.

'I've just come to see if you're coming home,' I said, trying to stay calm.

'Well you're out of luck, because I'm staying here,' she said, trying to close the door.

'What's wrong? Why are you treating me like this?' I asked.

'I've been seeing my old boyfriend at weekends,' she said. 'Now clear off, and don't bother coming back.'

I asked her if I could still visit Leoni, but she shut the door in my face. I got into my van and drove away, feeling stunned and foolish. It was obvious that she had planned this for some time. It was hard to believe that the same thing could happen three times to the same person.

For a couple of weeks I made several unsuccessful attempts to see Leoni. Each time I rang up or visited, there was always some excuse to stop me. The constant heartbreak over not seeing Leoni became too much for me to handle. To help me get through it, I started taking valium again. I gave up my struggle with Karen and decided to try and make a new life for myself.

With so many failed relationships behind me, my confidence was poor so I tried a dating agency. After being accepted I soon received a few replies. One lady from Bristol seemed to match up with my requirements, so I got in touch with her. After a week of telephone conversations, we agreed to meet.

The day before my date, a Christian lady I knew invited me to go to her church for tea. Although I had experienced some rejection from Christians already, I gave it a try. The tea was yet another disaster. Most people avoided me, possibly due to the fact they knew I'd been in prison. Their reaction made me feel dirty and uncomfortable. I was so fed up I was going to leave, when a young woman called Judith spoke to me.

'Are you enjoying yourself?' she asked.

'Not really,' I replied. 'I was about to go.'

She promised me a lift home if I'd stay for another half an hour. I admired her cheek, so I agreed. Over a coffee, we talked and got on quite well. She seemed quite different from the others, much more real. Out of everybody there, she was the only one who accepted me the way I was. When the thirty minutes were up, she drove me home as promised. On the way back she apologised for her friends behaviour, and asked me if I would come again.

'I doubt it,' I said. 'I've had enough rubbish off people to last me a lifetime.' I got out of the car and thanked her for being kind and understanding. By the next day, I'd forgotten her and the church, as I was excited about my date.

In the evening I drove to Bristol to meet her as arranged. It was the first time I'd been to the city since my transfer from Horfield Prison. After a successful evening, we agreed to see each other regularly. It wasn't very long before I was staying overnight. Within a few weeks I had moved in completely.

She had children of her own, which was fine except sometimes I felt excluded. Not satisfied with what I'd got, I began to pressurise her into having my baby. To try and influence her, I bought a car and started to shower her with expensive gifts. After months of pressure she realised she was pregnant.

'I hope you're satisfied now,' she said, crying.

Unfortunately I wasn't, as now I wanted us to get married. I was feeling so insecure about our relationship that I started having days off work. I spent them in the pub or in Devizes at my flat. Soon my money began to run out as I continued to spend lavishly.

My attitude towards her became aggressive as I couldn't get my own way. Finally she asked me to leave for a while so she could think things through. I returned to Devizes and got drunk for several days, while I waited for her to phone.

When I sobered up, I rang her to see if she was all right. She was very angry and distressed as she told me she'd lost the baby.

'What's happened,' I said anxiously. 'Please don't say you've got rid of it.'

'No I didn't,' she snapped, 'it got rid of itself. Now I want you out of my life for good.'

'Don't be like that,' I said, but it was too late, she'd already hung up.

Quickly I drove to her house, where I found my belongings already dumped on the pavement. After picking up my gear, I went to the off licence and bought several bottles of brandy. I sipped from a bottle as I drove back along the motorway to Devizes. By some miracle I arrived home without killing myself or anyone else. The journey from Bristol had only taken forty minutes, yet I was already a half a bottle down. I polished the rest of it off and fell asleep.

For the next two days all I could think of was the death of the unborn child. My feelings of guilt began to torture me. 'You're responsible for it's death, you murderer,' I said angrily to myself.

Every relationship I'd had I destroyed, even the one with Jesus. I couldn't bear the burden of my guilt any longer, so I tried to stab myself. Having lost all control, I left the flat and headed towards the canal to jump in. The knife was still in my hand, as I walked through the estate. Within minutes the police arrived and successfully persuaded me to give up the knife. As soon as it was in their hands they arrested me and led me to an awaiting car.

On the way to Chippenham nick, I cried out to Jesus for forgiveness, and hoped he would have me back. When we arrived at the station, the arresting officers were looking at me and laughing.

'You're history now Brian,' they said, 'we'll make sure of that.'

'But I haven't done anything,' I said, trying to defend myself.

'Carrying an offensive weapon with the intent to endanger life,' said the sergeant, 'that's pretty serious.'

'That's not right,' I said, complaining, 'I'm being stitched up.'

'I'll call the inspector to see what he says about it,' said the sergeant.

I sat against the wall in the cell-block, waiting for the inspector to arrive. When he did I was pleasantly surprised to find him kind and considerate. He asked me if I was all right, and would I be sensible if he released me. I told him that I had a lot of problems, but I promised him I'd sort them out properly. He told the officers to take me home and to forget the whole incident. Five minutes later I was on my way home.

'You're lucky it was him,' said the police driver, as he dropped me off. 'We call him the Christian cop, because he's very religous.'

Once I was safely indoors, I thanked Jesus for rescuing me, and promised him I wouldn't run away again. I felt better when I woke the following morning. For the first time in quite a while I didn't start the day by having a drink or taking any valium. I realised I couldn't survive as a Christian on my own any longer, so I asked God to send me some help.

A few days later my brother Philip called round and invited me to go to his baptism service. He had become a Christian a few weeks earlier during a special mission. He was getting baptised at the local swimming pool that evening, so I agreed to go along.

Philip was standing in the reception area when I arrived. He began to introduce me to his friends who were also getting baptised. I soon found out that his friends went to the church that had given me the brush off earlier. One of his friends was Judith the young lady who had been kind to me.

'We've met before haven't we?' asked Judith.

'Yes at your church tea,' I replied.

'Philip said he was going to see if you would come,' she said. 'I hope you won't find it as bad this time.'

I didn't as the service was a lively event, with everybody enjoying themselves. It was so good I agreed to go to the Sunday service. After a few weeks I started to go on a regular basis. It wasn't long before I got to know everyone quite well.

Judith and the Pastor ran the youth meetings, which were held at her flat on a Friday night. I started to attend them and finally agreed to help alternate weeks. One Friday when it was my turn, I was late leaving home, so I took the short cut to town. It was a badly lit road about half a mile long, with the canal on one side, and a dark wood on the other.

As I passed the last street light, I saw the figure of a man in front of me. This was a surprise, because it was rare to see anyone walking this way after dark. Drawing closer to the figure, I recognised it to be that of Glover. Hearing someone approaching him, he turned to take a look. When he did his face became a picture of terror as he saw it was me. For a second it looked like he was going to drop dead as his hands chutched his chest.

'He'd better not,' I thought, 'because I'm sure to get the blame if he does.'

He tried to call out, but the fear he was in made it impossible for the words to come out. His eyes revealed just how much he was afraid, as the tears started to run down his face. It was obvious that he was expecting me to take his life, just as I had promised.

'Please Brian don't kill me,' he stammered nervously. He closed his eyes expecting the worst.

Suddenly I was filled with compassion for him. The opportunity to kill him had come, but now I didn't want to. For the first time, I saw the terror from his point of view.

'Please don't be afraid,' I said softly. 'I'm not going to hurt you, I promise.'

'Why are you following me then?' he asked.

'I'm not,' I said, 'I just happen to be going the same way as you.'

We walked along the road together although he still kept his distance from me. I told about the events of my conversion, and how Jesus had changed me.

'Am I expected to believe that,' said Glover.

'I know it sounds crazy,' I said, 'but it is true. If it wasn't you would be dead.'

'That's true,' he said, feeling relieved.

'I'm sorry for all the things I've done to you,' I said. 'I forgive you, will you please forgive me?'

'OK I will,' he replied.

I gave him a friendly hug, and invited him for a drink. We went into a pub where everyone knew of the hostility between us. Putting my arm around him I publicly declared the end of my vendetta against him. Now I'd made peace with my enemy, I was feeling on top of the world. After a few drinks, I said goodbye to Glover, leaving him to celebrate by himself. I arrived at Judith's flat too late for the meeting, but in time for coffee. I apologised for being late and tried to explain why.

'Something unexpected cropped up,' I said.

'Yes it smells like it,' said the pastor grinning.

'Oh the drink,' I said, realising what he was getting at. 'That's part of the reason.'

'If you say so,' he said, unconvinced.

I was determined not give up, so I carried on telling Judith about my meeting with Glover. The teenagers who attended the youth meeting became interested and stayed on to ask questions. From then on Judith and I spent most nights talking to the kids about Jesus. Working together with them, meant that Judith and I became very close friends. As the weeks went by our feelings for each other deepened, until we spent all our time together. We hadn't planned to be emotionally involved, but it appeared God had other ideas. It became obvious to us and our friends, that God was pushing us together. Finally during Christmas we decided that we did love each other. After two weeks praying together, we felt God was directing us to get married. Confident we'd made the right decision, we set a date in May for the wedding.

In the hope of having Leoni for a bridesmaid, I contacted Karen. I was really surprised when she agreed, and shocked when she offered me unlimited access to Leoni. After a year of uncertainty, it started to look like my troubles were over.

Chapter Eleven

THE OCCULT

It wasn't long before I was in trouble again, only it was trouble of a different kind.

I was taking my Alsatian dog Luke, for a run over Roundway Downs, at night in the van. The Downs are a large range of hills overlooking Devizes. It was also the site of a very famous battle, during the Civil War, between the Roundheads and the Royalists.

It was just after midnight, when I reached the top of the hill. I drove across the track leading to the other side, where there was a picnic area. From this viewpoint, you could see everything clearly for several miles. It was a bright and clear night as the moon was pretty full. The quiet tranquil surroundings made it a good place to pray.

I let the dog out of the van, and looked to see if there was anyone else around. When I was certain that I was alone, I knelt down and started to pray. I had hardly said a word before I was interrupted by a strange humming noise. I looked up but there was nothing there, so I just ignored it and carried on praying.

The humming noise grew louder until it was all around me, making its presence felt. Before I had chance to react, it was upon me. I started to feel cold and clammy all over as it wrapped itself around me. I tried to fight it off, but I couldn't see it, only feel it's powerful grip crushing me. The force was so strong, that my lungs started to burn as the air was squeezed out of them. I was confused and started to think I was going mad.

'Who are you, and what do you want?' I shouted, trying to communicate with it. Of course there was no answer, just the continuing assault on my body. A mixture of anger and fear filled me, as I struggled hopelessly to get free. I had never been afraid of anybody or anything, but this was something different. My attacker this time was definitely not of this world.

All my strength was gone, so I gave up the struggle and waited for the end to come. Then a voice kept telling me to pray.

'Jesus, Jesus,' I cried, 'please help me.'

He must have heard me, because at that very moment the vice-like grip let go. I was surprised, but I wasn't about to ask questions how he managed it. As fast as my legs would carry me, I scrambled into the van and drove off at lightning speed.

Half way across the track I remembered that I had left the dog behind. I looked in the mirror and saw him running after me. It was just as well he was, because I didn't have any intention of going back for him.

The end of the track was in sight now, so I felt safe enough to stop and let him catch up.

'Come on Luke, hurry up!' I shouted, opening the door for him. As he jumped inside, the humming sound approached again.

'This is crazy,' I cried, 'it's actually chasing me.' Before I could get going again, the force had closed in. Once again my fear ran into panic and I fumbled with the gears. The van came under attack, and started to shake. The noise became deafening as it drew up alongside me. It seemed as if it was about to strike and drag me off to devour me. It was as if the whole of the hill had come to life and was rising up against me. It was definitely hunting me, like a beast chasing it's prey. Unfortunately I was the prey.

'Why me?' I yelled at my attacker, 'what have I done to you?' Once more I called out to God, 'Lord help me, save me!' I cried.

Suddenly I felt calm and I managed to get the van into gear. Once more I put my foot to the floor, and drove like a maniac. Doing forty across a track full of potholes wasn't doing the van much good, but I didn't care.

'Thank you Lord,' I said with relief, as I reached the end of the track. The presence of the force faded out, as I started my descent back down the hill. Looking back towards the top of the hill, I thought I saw something, or someone standing there. The further I got away from the hill the better I felt.

During the attack, I had suffered extreme punishment, yet there were no lasting effects from it. I was still quite afraid, even after getting home. I started to become paranoid, thinking that it might have followed me home. I decided to take no chances, so I began to prepare some defences. I had no idea what shape or form my potential attacker might take. With this in mind I decided that who or whatever came to the door, I would consider them my mortal enemy.

In the hallway was the dog, who was my first line of defence. I didn't have much confidence in him though, because he'd seemed disinterested on the hill. I put more trust in steel, so under my pillow I put a nine inch bayonet, along with my Bible.

'If anyone comes Luke,' I said to my dog. 'I'll set you on them, and then stick them with the bayonet. If that fails then I'll resort to the Bible.'

However the night passed by without any further trouble. In the morning I pondered on the nights events; it was all beyond human reasoning. After praying about it, I felt that it was in response to my dramatic conversion. It was as though someone was trying to stop me from continuing as a Christian. I kept all of this to myself, because I didn't feel anyone would believe me.

A few days later I received a letter, which had been delivered by hand. The letter itself was rather strange, especially as it was anonymous. It's content suggested that it came from a religous person. Whoever it was, spoke of how important I was to them, and how they were still interested in me. I found it quite flattering as I wasn't used to receiving personal mail.

I decided to show it to some of the people at the church, to see what they thought of it. The leaders of the church, thought it a little strange, but said it was harmless. Feeling reassured I kept it and returned home.

Later that night I was sitting in the lounge reading the Bible, when a humming noise started up. It was coming from the direction of the window. It was the same eerie humming noise I'd heard on the hill. I walked towards the window to get a better look, when suddenly a powerful force burst inside. It came straight through the window, as if the glass was made of plastic. I was driven back forcibly towards the wall, and a clammy coldness came over me.

Somehow I managed to get free and run outside. When I was safely out of the flat, my fear turned to anger.

'I'm not going to be driven out of my home,' I said angrily.

I plucked up courage and nervously went back inside. I was relieved to find that everything was normal back in the living room.

For a couple of days I was shaken and confused, but with the help of few stiff drinks I soon forgot it. A week later, another letter arrived in the same way. It read pretty much the same as the other one, except that it's tone was more forceful. Whoever had written it said that they were going to make me part of their family. Once again they had failed to sign it. I began to be annoyed and irritated by whoever they were. 'Lord show me what's going on,' I prayed, 'and who this is.'

There was a youth meeting that night which I was sharing in, so once again I forgot all about it. The meeting had lasted a long time, so it was quite late when I arrived home. I had only been inside a few minutes when the eerie noise sounded from outside the living room window.

I could only look on with horror as the force entered the room in the same manner as before. It was upon me before I had chance to move. Fearfully I called on the name of the Lord Jesus to help me. The noise intensified, and the force grasped me. It seemed intent on trying to terrify or destroy me. I wanted to run away, but a calming voice told me to trust the Lord, and stand my ground.

I reached out for my bible, and held it tightly to my chest. Falling to my knees, I started praying all different prayers. For twenty minutes the evil force continued to pressurise me, but somehow I was still hanging on.

'You'll have to kill me, because I'm not moving,' I said angrily towards my attacker. 'And in the name of Jesus Christ I order you to get out of my house. I didn't really understand what I was praying as it just seemed to come out of my mouth. Whatever it was, it appeared to work, as immediately after that, the force left. It went in the same manner as it had come, like a powerful wind being driven along.

It was a relief to be free, as the force had almost squeezed the life out of me. It was also a privilage to have witnessed such power from God in delivering me from an unseen enemy. I sat on the sofa feeling exhausted from my ordeal. However I couldn't rest as I was too confused, so I asked God to help me to understand.

'What does it all mean?' I asked, 'and why?'

Instantly the answer was revealed. The key to the problem was the letters. It was so obvious, I couldn't understand why I hadn't realised before. The letters were some kind of messenger, which allowed the evil force to gain access into my home. Convinced of there influence, I decided that they had to be destroyed.

I picked them up and went to the end of our road, where I set fire to them. I watched as they disintergrated in the flames, and the ashes disappeared into the night sky. It seemed a bit bizarre to go to such lengths but I was taking no chances. I didn't know whether what I had done was right or not, but it certainly made me feel better. The next day I told Judith about it, and she advised me to talk to some friends of hers. They were a couple from Ipswich, called Ken and Chris, who were visiting our church.

I talked it over with them, and we decided to have a special prayer time to make sure everything had gone. The next day we got together as arranged and prayed for an insight into the situation. After half an hour had passed, a picture began to form in my mind. It was a picture of a large sword, the type used in medieval times by knights.

'That might mean the scriptures as they are known as the sword of the spirit, said Ken.

'It's not a sword for good, but for evil,' I said.

We continued to pray, and as we did the picture I saw expanded. It was now showing the sword in the hand of a knight, who was dressed in full armour.

'I've got it,' I said excitedly. 'The knight was a crusader.'

'You'll have to explain,' said Ken. 'I don't know what you mean.'

'Eight years ago after being ill, I got involved with a group of spiritualists.'

'Did you hold services?' asked Ken.

'Sort of,' I replied. 'Although it was more like a ritual or a seance, than a service. There was no prayers or singing, only chanting and humming.'

The memory of my time with the group came flooding back, and for a moment I felt I was reliving it.

'Take your time,' said Chris.

I was worried that I might encounter the evil force again, if I carried on talking about it.

'You're safe here,' said Ken reassuringly.

After a few minutes prayer I continued with my account of the cult group. 'As I got more involved with them, I was introduced to their leader. He was supposed to have special powers to heal and predict the future. When I met him, I was surprised because he looked so ordinary.'

'What did you expect to see?' asked Ken.

'I don't know, maybe someone dressed in a hooded gown,' I said with a laugh. 'Anyway the leader and I stood in the centre of the room, while all the others made a circle around us. Then everybody placed their hands on me and started chanting. After a while the leader went into a trance and started speaking to me. "I see a clock with no hands, which represents no time limit for your health. Also you are going to receive some special letters in the future." 'When, and what about?' I asked.

'I'm afraid I can't say where their from, or when it will happen,' he said.

As I got to the last part of my story, my breathing became rapid and I started to feel a pain in my chest. Everone prayed for me, and after a while I was able to continue.

'The leader put his hand on my head and told me I'd been given a companion, who would never leave me.

'I can see him standing behind you now,' he said. 'He's your crusader dressed in his armour, ready to serve you.'

'Immediately after he said this, I said. 'I felt a strong presence behind me and a heaviness on my back making it hard to breathe. The next day when I was having a bath, I touched my breastbone and was sent into a nervous spasm.

'You've had it all this time, have you?' asked Chris.

'It disappeard for a while when I was in prison, but returned just before my conversion.'

'I believe the crusader is an evil spirit, who wants to either control you, or destroy you,' said Ken.

'That makes sense,' I said.

'All we need to do is to get rid of it,' said Ken cheerfully.

'It sounds too easy,' I said, getting worried.

We sat and read several Bible verses, which were relevant to the situation. We prayed for guidance in the way we should go about a deliverance. Firstly I had to renounce any allegiance I may have had to the occult.

Ken ordered the evil spirit to leave in the name of Jesus Christ, and never return.

I found that receiving deliverance was basically the same as receiving salvation. The main ingredient was for me to want freedom, and say I was sorry. I felt frightened as the conflict between good and evil battled within me. I began to shake and sweat as a stabbing pain moved through me.

'Get out of my life, in the name of Jesus Christ,' I screamed.

During the struggle we continued to recite the Bible verse we'd been given by God. 'Whatever you bind on earth will be bound in heaven, and whatever you loose on earth will be loosed in heaven.'

After another five minutes of constant prayer, the conflict was over and the battle was won.

It felt as though my shoulder-blades had been broken, pulled back and reset. The weight on my back had gone completely, and my lungs were able to expand fully for the first time in ages. The tightness and the nervous reaction in my chest was now gone forever.

The truth about the cult had been revealed to me. They seemed pleasant enough on the outside, with good intentions, but inside they were like venomous snakes. Although the influence of the occult had been broken, it had left it's scars on me. The pressure of those last few weeks meant that I was now pumping more valium down my throat than normal.

Chapter Twelve

ADDICTION

Because I'd been taking more valium recently, I soon found my prescriptions running out. Immediately I was on the phone to the doctor's surgery, to order some more.

I was told that repeat prescriptions were not being given without seeing the doctor first.

'What's the problem?' I asked, 'I've been receiving these drugs for years.'

'You'll have to make an appointment,' said the receptionist. 'It's doctors orders.'

I was given an appointment for the following week, which wasn't too bad as I always had a reserve stock. These were kept in the airing cupboard, which had been a hiding place for all my contraband. It was a particularily good place for drugs, as it was so warm and dry. Many times it had been used for storing and drying cannabis.

I opened the door, and pulled out the biscuit tin which contained my supply. After the first few bottles I took out, were empty my search turned into a desperate panic.

'Come on, where are you,' I shouted, as I tipped out the contents of the tin onto the floor.

With great relief I came across a bottle of valium half full. Emptying the pills out, I became calm again as I worked out that I had enough to last until I saw the doctor. It was a shock to find all the other bottles empty, because three months earlier they had been full. I searched through the flat, hoping to find the missing pills, but found nothing.

It didn't take me long to work out what had happened to them. I knew I'd taken them myself, I just didn't want to admit to it. At my worst times, I'd been taking between seventy and a hundred milligrams a day. It had got so bad that I'd lost count of how much I was taking.

'If my habit's got that bad,' I thought, 'I'll never survive on the three-hundred pills a month I get now.

No one at the church knew of my drug habit, not even Judith. It wasn't something I felt I could share with anyone. I was afraid that if I told them I was a junkie, they would reject me.

I decided that I had no choice but to tell Judith. The date for our wedding had been set, and I couldn't start married life with that secret. That night I went to Judith's flat determined to tell her of my habit. She looked worried when I told her I had a confession to make.

'I'm a drug addict,' I said nervously, 'and I have been for many years. The pills you've seen me taking are valium.'

'Valium?' cried Judith, 'but you told me they were for a sinus condition.'

'I know, I'm sorry,' I said feeling ashamed. 'I was lying, but only because I didn't think you'd have time for a junkie.'

She was sympathetic and tried to understand why I hadn't been able to confide in her. However when she asked me how much I was taking, I found myself lying again. I assured her it was under control and that I was seeing the doctor the following week.

'Will you ask him, to start reducing your dosage?' asked Judith.

'Yes, that's why I'm seeing him,' I said, lying again.

I felt awful as I walked home. I had gone there to be honest about my habit, but only succeeded in being more deceitful. As for cutting down on my dose, I didn't have a lot of choice.

My appointment with the doctor soon arrived, and I was wondering what I could say to him. I hoped he wouldn't ask where my pills had gone, because I certainly didn't have an answer.

'Mr Russ, do come in,' he said with a smile.

'He's in a good mood, maybe my lucks changed,' I thought.

'Now what seems to be the trouble,' he said.

'Oh no trouble doctor,' I said lying. 'It's just that your secretary said I had to see you if I wanted some valium.'

'I'll just check your records, wouldn't want you to get addicted would we,' he said laughing.

'If only he knew,' I thought.

'It looks like you've had your ration for this month,' he said. 'Yes here it is, you had your last prescription a week ago.'

'I did,' I said, sounding astonished.

'Have you used all those already?' he asked.

'No, I've made a mistake,' I said, trying to talk my way out of it. 'I must have got the bottles mixed up.'

'I'll see you in four weeks time then,' he said, 'when your prescription is due.

I walked out of the surgery feeling very dejected. I couldn't believe that I hadn't told him the truth.

I walked down the canal towpath and sat down under the bridge. Taking out my bottle of valium, I counted out the remainder of my pills.

'They won't last me four days, let alone four weeks,' I said in despair.

The only place I could get some more, was on the black market, but my finances wouldn't allow that. For a moment I thought about doing a robbery, but I quickly dismissed it.

The situation had become desperate, and my future was looking doubtful. With all this racing through my mind, I started to think of killing myself. 'I'm probably going to die anyway,' I said looking at my reflection in the water.

Drowning was a better alternative than dying in agony. The idea of having to face cold turkey, didn't appeal to me at all.

'Is there any other way out of this mess?' I asked God. 'Surely this is too difficult even for you.'

I took out my little pocket Bible, and started to read from where it fell open. It said that I wouldn't come to any harm, but I had hope and a future. I felt the Lord tell me, I had to stop taking the drugs or face certain death. He promised to lead me through the dark times I had ahead of me. I knew he was right about me dying, as I'd been feeling ill for quite a long time. I promised God that I wouldn't take any more pills, but trust in him to keep me from harm.

Over the next few days, my health got worse, but I still managed to keep it from everyone. Finally I had no choice but to tell everyone at church, after I collapsed during a meeting.

'Look I'm a drug addict, and five days ago I quit taking them,' I said trembling.

'Did you think we wouldn't find out?' asked one of the leaders.

'I thought I could handle it alone,' I said.

'You can't just stop like that,' said a lady who was a nurse. 'You'll die or go mad.'

I felt discouraged by what had been said, but it was only the same as what I'd thought myself. Although no one in the church knew how to help me, they continued to pray for me. I decided to keep a diary, so as the days went by, I could chart my progress. It had been ten days since I last took any valium. The sickness and violent cramps were getting more frequent.

I agreed to go to the evening service with Judith, as the leaders told me I might feel better. The service hadn't been going long, before I was out of my chair and rolling on the floor. The pain got worse as I fought to get my breath. Everyone was staring at me, because my groaning and coughing was louder than their singing. Finally to save them and myself further embarrassment, I came out of the service. The pain I was in was so severe that I had to crawl to the car.

All my muscles tightened up and started to go into spasms, making breathing even more difficult. The whole of my system moved up a gear, as the adrenalin pumped wildly through me. In a moment of madness, I tried to knock myself out, by head-butting the steering wheel.

'Why don't you do something to help me God,' I screamed. Coming to my senses, I turned and looked towards the church hall, where the service was in full swing.

'They seem to be enjoying themselves,' I thought, as I watched them singing and dancing.

Feelings of despair and rejection filled me, as they continued whooping it up. My distress turned to anger as I started to voice my complaint to God.

'How can they carry on like that, when I'm out here fighting for my life,' I said. 'I'm sorry Lord, I don't mean to be cross, but it doesn't seem very fair.'

I wondered whether God could hear me above all their singing. I didn't know if he was in there listening to them or out in the car with me. For a while my symptoms went, and I became calm and restful. The word peace stuck in my mind. The short respite God provided me with, gave me the strength I needed to carry on. I went back to Judith's flat to wait for her. I felt that I had been deserted by the others, so I wasn't keen on seeing them.

When Judith returned I was already going through another bad spell. We fought the addiction together in prayer. It was a tough job, which was beginning to drain both of us.

As the panic set in, my first reaction was to reach for the brandy bottle. I filled a pint glass half full with brandy, and emptied it with one swallow. I hoped it would slow down my adrenalin, but it made it faster instead.

'Try and hold on,' said Judith pleading.

'I can't, it's too much,' I said getting paranoid. Feeling more afraid than before, I ran from the flat and got into my car. I drove towards the hospital, and parked in a side street nearby. Although I knew God was with me, to be by the hospital made me feel a little more secure.

I didn't know if I would make it through the night, but my survival instincts kept me praying. Finally around three o'clock I fell asleep for a few hours.

Judith was at work all the next day, which meant I was on my own. Apart from God, she was my only other support, as I probably frightened everyone else away. I hadn't eaten for several days, and I was beginning to feel exhausted.

By the time Judith got home, I had gone into cold turkey further. We rang up Ken and Chris in Ipswich, to see if they could help. They immediately agreed to let me stay for a few days. Neither of them were working, so they were able to offer me round the clock support. The next day Judith and I set off for Ipswich, arriving late in the evening. The journey had been exhausting for me, as my body continued to shake and have involuntary spasms.

Shortly after our arrival we prayed, and Ken gave me several verses of the Bible to meditate on. For the whole evening we prayed and by ten o'clock I was feeling quite relaxed. I went to bed and slept all night for the first time in a week. I got up the next morning to find Judith had already returned to Devizes, because she had to work. After breakfast, Ken took me to a marina, to have a look at the boats. I began to get suspicious when we moved from dry land to a floating walkway.

'Where are we going Ken?' I asked anxiously, as I followed him across the floating path.

'Nowhere really,' he said, 'I just thought you might like a little walk.'

I looked back along the snaking path towards the shoreline, which was getting further away. The water licked up around the path, as if it were trying to swallow it. I started to pray very hard, especially as I couldn't swim. Ken was marching away on the wooden path, making it sway about.

I started to panic, and called out to Ken for help. He turned towards me and reached out his hand.

'It's all right Brian, I've got you,' he said in a calming voice. He lead me back to shore and we drove home. On the way back he told me why he'd taken me out onto the watery path.

'I just wanted to encourage you to pray,' he said.

After lunch, Ken and Chris went to visit a relative, leaving me alone in the house. After a while I started to feel afraid, as my mind began to play tricks on me. I started to wonder whether I'd ever see Judith or Leoni again. As the paranoia increased I decided to go to the shops and get some beer. When I reached the door, I found I was too afraid to go any further than the step. As it was raining quite hard, I turned to go back inside, and found I couldn't do that either. For two hours I sat on the step in the rain, until Ken and Chris returned to rescue me.

I spent most of the next couple of days, praying and meditating on various scriptures. The more I prayed and read the Bible the better I became, until the spasms stopped altogether.

At the end of the week I was ready to make the return journey to Devizes. Ken and I met Judith at a service station twenty miles north of London. After a coffee and a prayer we went our separate ways. On the way back to London Judith became ill, so I had to drive. As darkness fell, we approached the M25 that took us round London. The volume of traffic increased, and so did their speed. I began to find it difficult to cope, because my mind wasn't working properly. The traffic appeared to be travelling far quicker than it really was, and very soon I was freaking out.

'Can you drive please Judith,' I begged.

Judith didn't hear me, as she was fast asleep from her illness. After another two miles of paranoia, I was about to open the car door to jump out. I found myself shouting: For God has not given me a spirit of fear, but Power, Love and sound mind. From that moment on, the journey was peaceful.

Within a few weeks of returning home, I was drug free, and healthy. God had completely healed me by the time our wedding arrived. It was a great day for Judith and I, and having Leoni there as bridesmaid. After a brief honeymoon period, I got down to some serious work, both for me and for God.

Chapter Thirteen

TRUST ME

I started working for myself, buying and selling goods from auctions, and doing house clearances. At weekends when I didn't see Leoni, Judith and I would work on my stall at Bath market.

After several months hard work, I'd accumulated three garage's full of bric a brac, furniture, and other items. The harder I worked, the more it grew, until I didn't have room for any more.

I owed over two thousand pounds in total, mainly to the Bank and the council for rent arrears. Although I was trying to pay them off, I wasn't very regular with the payments. Finally the council gave me notice to quit the garages.

For a while I rented some space in a barn just outside Devizes. After two months I had to move out, when the roof blew off during a storm. As I looked for new premises, I noticed that the council hadn't yet taken back my old garages. In desperation, I crammed all my gear into them, and hoped no one would notice.

I only needed to use them for a few days, as I had planned to sell all my stock at the next auction. Several weeks passed by and I still hadn't sold it, as I wanted to get a better price. Then a man I knew in the trade, agreed to take everything for a quarter of it's value. When he came to collect it I found the garage empty and swept clean. That very day the council had repossessed the garage, taking all my stock to the tip.

I spent the next day shouting angrily at the council, without any success. Finally I gave up and turned my anger towards God instead. 'Why have you let this happen?' I asked. Opening my Bible I read the first thing I saw. It advised me against storing up material wealth, because it doesn't last. It was true, I could have sold the stock at any time, but I preferred to get a higher price. After saying I was sorry to God for the mess I was in, he helped me sort out my debts.

Just before Christmas I started thinking about the plight of the homeless. While I was praying for them generally, I felt God tell me to feed the poor and homeless in Devizes. I had no idea how I was supposed to go about this task, but I knew if it was what God wanted, it would work out.

I put an advertisement in the local paper to say there would be a lunch provided on Christmas day for those who were needy. Having secured a venue, Judith and I started to ask shops and churches for donations.

With only a week left until the lunch, it seemed impossible yet I was overwhelmed with goods. Everytime I went into a shop they showered me with food, as though I'd been expected. Offers of help came from various christians, from all different churches.

On Christmas Eve we prepared everything for the next day, still not sure if anyone would turn up. I looked at the mountain of food and gifts that had been provided, and wondered if it would go. Christmas Day arrived, and with it came about thirty people. It was a great success. Not only did everyone have lunch but they all took a small hamper home as well. One homeless lad called Pete remained behind after everyone else had gone. Judith and I invited him to stay with us until he found somewhere permanent to live.

Shortly after Christmas we had a few friends round for supper and a video. At the end of the evening I gave them a lift home, leaving Pete and Judith to clear up. I left the door on the latch as I was only going to be ten minutes. When I returned I found the police inside talking to Judith and Pete.

'We've had an armed gang in here,' said Pete.

'He's right ' said Judith, tearfully. 'There were three of them, all in masks and carrying iron bars.'

'Was anything taken?' asked the police sergeant.

'No, nothing,' replied Judith, 'they just asked Pete about some money from Bristol.'

I became angry at the thought of someone invading my home and threatening my wife. I felt guilty that I wasn't here to protect and guard my territory.

'Do you think someone is out to get you Brian?' asked the sergeant.

'Why do you say that?' I said.

'Well you must have made a few enemies over the years,' he said.

'Whoever did this will pay very dearly, I said, making a promise. Because the police believed the gang would return, they advised Judith to spend the night elsewhere.

'If they come back Brian ring us straight away,' said the sergeant.

I went to the cupboard and took out a pick-axe handle. 'If they do come back, they'll be sorry,' I said.

'I haven't seen that,' he said. 'Defend yourself by all means, but don't kill them.'

After the police had gone, I dropped Judith off at a friends house and then returned home. Pete and I sat up all night waiting for the armed gang to come back, but they never did. In the morning the CID came round and took our statements. One of the detectives called DS Oliver took me into the kitchen and asked for my help.

'You know the right people to ask,' he said. 'I'm sure you'll be able to persuade someone to tell you who did it.'

'And if I do, what then?' I asked.

'Let us know, and we'll do the rest,' he said.

It wasn't long before I was out knocking on doors finding out what I wanted to know. Most people I asked were willing to co-operate, but one or two needed a little bit of persuasion. By nine o'clock that night, I had the names and addresses of the people involved in the attack.

I wasn't surprised to find Pete's name being mentioned, but I didn't know how he was linked to it. He disappeared before I had the chance to confront him with it. I held onto the information, while I considered whether to deal with the gang myself or not. After thinking about it all night, I decided to co-operate with the police.

The next day I went to the station to pass on the names I'd been given. While I was there they asked me to listen to a tape they'd been given. It was a telephone conversation between a man and the Avon and Somerset police force. He was telling them about £40,000 that had been stolen from a post-office in Gloucester.

'What have you got to say about that then Brian?' asked DS Oliver.

'I don't know,' I said, feeling confused. 'Is it supposed to mean something to me?'

'Don't you think the voice on the tape sounds a bit like you,' said DC Jones. 'He's got the same accent as you.'

'There must be thousands of people with that accent,' I said.

'We just thought you might know a bit more than you've told us,' said DS Oliver.

'You think I'm mixed up in all this don't you?' I asked.

'Who knows?' said DS Oliver, shrugging his shoulders. 'You can go now, we know where you are if we need you.'

On the way home I started to pray, something I hadn't done much of since the robbery. Slowly I realised I had been trying to sort out my troubles myself. When I got home I apologised to Judith for being selfish. We prayed together asking for forgiveness and help to forgive the men who had broken in. That night we slept peacefully for the first time since the attack.

Two days later the police told us that the men had confessed to the crime. The truth of the story finally came out. Pete was the main culprit because he told the gang he'd stole £40,000 from the post-office. He had invented the story to gain respect from the gang. They thought he had hidden the money in our flat, and decided to snatch it when I was out.

The whole thing had taught me that relying on my own strength was not the best way. I had thought it was a sign of weakness if I didn't do something about it. From the moment the attack took place, my thoughts were of revenge and nothing else.

In the Bible, Jesus taught his disciples to turn the other cheek, when they were attacked. As violence had always played a big part in my life, it was difficult for me. Now after our recent experience I asked God to make my attitude the same as Jesus.

After only two days, my first test came. Judith and I were asleep in bed, when we woke to hear the dog barking loudly. He was going crazy because someone was kicking and banging our door. Whoever it was began to shout abuse through the letterbox. I got dressed and went to see who it was. I held onto the dog, and opened the door. Two angry looking men who smelled of drink were standing there.

'What's your problem?' I snapped.

'Your dog's barking at us,' he replied.

'Of course he's barking at you, you idiot,' I said, getting mad. 'You're trying to kick my door in.'

They took a step towards me and began to make threats. I looked at the pick-axe handle that was still behind the door, and thought about using it on them. Before I did, I found myself apologizing for the dog barking at them.

'I can't believe I said that,' I thought. Apologizing was the last thing on my mind. They looked a little shocked for a while, but then they raised their fists and threatened me again.

Once more I considered hitting them with the pick-axe handle, but instead out of my mouth came something else.

'I'm sorry if I've offended you,' I said.

They were as horrified as I was at that statement, and took a step backwards. I realised that God was taking charge of me, and of them.

Finally they came forward and went to throw a punch at me. I stood still and dropped my hands. I told them I wasn't going to defend myself and they could do what they liked.

I waited for the blows to strike me, but instead I found them fall back. To my amazement they started apologizing to me, and begged me to forgive them. After I had, they left very slowly, apologizing and grovelling all the way.

Afterwards Judith and I prayed and thanked God for his protection. He had showed me that it was possible to turn the other cheek and still be victorious.

Within a few weeks I had another opportunity to put it to the test. It was a Saturday night and Judith and I had been having a row about going to church. I wanted to go to a car boot sale in the morning to sell a few antiques I had. There had been quite a few problems at church lately and I didn't want to be involved. Unable to agree with her, I loaded up the van, and told her I wouldn't be back.

I decided to have a drink in the pub to cool off a bit before going back home to apologise. I hadn't been there long, when three people I knew came in and stood next to me. The man in the centre wore a long black coat and a large black hat. He had been involved in the occult for quite some time.

'I see you've made the headlines again Brian,' he said.

I shrugged my shoulders in response, as I wasn't interested in talking to him.

'I hope you're not starting to oppose me,' he said, in a threatening manner.

I didn't know what he meant by it, and I didn't want to know, so I ignored him and walked away. He walked after me and continued to make his threats.

'Look, I've just come out for a quiet drink,' I said, beginning to lose my patience.

'Christianity is rubbish, and so is Jesus Christ,' he said, with a snarl.

I realised it was foolish to get into a debate with him, so I moved away again.

'I am stronger than your Jesus,' he said boastfully, as he followed me once more.

'You won't get away with mocking God forever,' I said, beginning to make a stand.

'The power in me is stronger than in Christ,' he cried.

'You're mad,' I said. 'You'll never be stronger than him.'

'Let's put it to the test then,' he said grinning, as he reached out his hand towards me.

'Get lost,' I shouted, 'I'm not getting involved in any of your games.'

'Let me give you one of my blessings,' he said, trying to place his hand on my head.

I backed away feeling a little scared as I knew that his blessings were really curses. With a few yards between us, I quietly asked God to show me what I should do. I felt God wanted me to speak to my enemy using Bible verses.

I couldn't believe that God wanted me to quote the Bible in the pub on a Saturday night. I prayed a second time, and once again I received the same message. By this time the man in black was standing in front of me again.

'You can't stop me, can you?' he said, trying to grab hold me. 'I told you I had more power than your God.'

'Help me Jesus,' I cried.

I tried desperately to push his hand away from me, but he was very strong. Then suddenly without thinking I started reciting Bible verses at him. It appeared as if my mouth was a cannon, as word after word shot out at my attacker. They certainly had power as the man in black was knocked backwards. He turned and retreated towards the exit, where he faced me once again.

Full of confidence, I walked towards him and continued to recite the Bible at him. He staggered backwards once again, and ran out of the door. His face showed an expression of horror, as he fled cursing and swearing.

I was too embarrassed to go back into the bar, so I went into the lounge instead. I bought another drink and sat down to try to work out what had happened.

While I sat there, God told me to pray, because my attacker had placed a curse upon me and my van.

I decided to finish my drink first, as I didn't think it would matter when I prayed. By the time I'd drunk it, I'd forgotten all about praying.

I left the pub and got into my van and started driving the half a mile home. I hadn't gone far when God reminded me I hadn't prayed about the curse.

'Lord I'm sorry,' I said starting to pray. 'Please forgive me for not taking notice of your warning. In the name of Jesus Christ, I bind up that curse and command it to return to the man in black.'

When I had finished praying I looked in the mirror to find I was being followed by a police car. Although I'd only had two drinks in the pub, it was possible I might be over the limit.

'Lord I'm sorry for drinking and driving,' I cried. 'You know it wasn't my intention. I'm not trying to make excuses, but I just forgot in all the drama. Please forgive me and keep me from harm.'

I stopped the van and got out after the police car flashed his lights at me. There was only one policeman present and he came and stood right next to me. He asked if he could look inside the van, as there had been several burglaries that day. I opened the back doors of the van and watched him search through my antiques. He accepted my explanation for carrying the antiques and closed the door.

'Everything seems to be in order,' he said. 'Anything in the front of the van?'

'I don't think so,' I said.

'Can I look?' he asked.

'Yes of course,' I said.

As soon as I'd agreed, I realised it was a mistake. I had forgotten that on the floor of the passenger side was a swordstick. I had got it from a house clearance several months earlier. It was worth about a hundred pounds but it was illegal to carry it around. In my haste to get away from home I had taken it with me. My heart beat faster as he went to open the door.

'It's locked,' he said, 'can you unlock it for me.'

'Yes alright,' I said, sadly.

'Don't bother,' he said, 'you can go.'

He got into his car and drove off, leaving me feeling shocked but happy. All the way home I thanked God for looking after me, and promised to go to church the next day. It was a bizarre tale to tell Judith when I got home, but at least it helped us forget our troubles.

A few days later I received some news about the man from the pub. He had been drinking heavily at a hotel before driving home. As he turned into his driveway a police car pulled in behind him. He failed the breathalyser and was charged with drinking and driving.

When I had prayed about the curse he'd put upon me, it went back and landed on him. It really showed me just how great God is, and if I trusted him completely, nothing was impossible.

Sadly shortly after, the good that had happened was over-shadowed by the rift in the church. Eventually the division got worse and finally the church split in two.

Chapter Fourteen

ALBERT

The split in the church left a lot of people feeling bitter and unhappy. The grumbling and fault-finding continued as everyone tried to reason it out.

I understood the anger that some people felt, but personally I found it difficult to live with. After trying unsuccessfully to bring about peace, we left, and got on with our lives. Now we were temporarily without a church, I began to wonder whether God would use me or not. In spite of that, our lives continued to improve in every department.

My access with Leoni had increased, as she was now allowed to stay with us on every other weekend. My job was better paid and only part-time, leaving me plenty of free time, but still no work from God. One day as I returned home from dropping Leoni at Karen's, I was given my task. 'I want you to go and see Albert,' said a powerful distinct voice from inside the van.

'Go and see Albert,' I said, a bit startled, 'Albert who?' Instantly a picture of a man I used to know, called Albert formed in my mind.

'If that's you speaking Lord, make it clear,' I said boldly.

That evening at home, I was in the bathroom shaving, when once again I heard the message. 'Brian, are you going to see Albert, or not?' said the voice loudly.

'All right I'm going,' I said, 'I just wanted to make sure it was you, that's all.'

I left straight away and soon arrived outside the house of the only Albert I knew. It had been several years since I'd visited him and his wife, as I used to call round with my cousin. They both kept pigeons, and they shared the same loft. For many years Albert had suffered badly with his health, and hadn't been able to work for over ten years. He had sufferered with asthma for fifteen years, and been a cancer patient for nine. On top of that, he'd suffered six heart attacks.

'Lord, I don't know what you've got in mind here, but I'm willing,' I said, as I walked up the path.

'Come in Brian,' said Albert's wife, 'we haven't seen you for a long time.'

'I've come to see Albert, if that's all right,' I said.

'He's not been well for six months,' she said, 'but he'll be pleased to see you.'

When I went into the lounge, Albert was having some oxygen from his portable machine.

'I've heard that you've become religous,' said Albert taking away his mask.

'I don't know about that,' I said, jokingly, 'but I have become a Christian.'

'Well, I wouldn't have thought that possible,' he said.

'Your wife tells me you've have a tough time recently,' I said.

'Yeah, I've almost had enough,' he said sadly. 'I don't know why I keep fighting it, really.'

In between taking his oxygen, he told me how he'd almost died from a tumour in his lungs. Luckily they were able to shrink it with a laser, but it had left him virtually disabled.

'Can't you move around at all?' I asked.

'Not really,' he said. 'It takes me over an hour to get upstairs at night. When I finally reach the top step, I have to stop for half an hour until I get my breath back.'

He stopped talking for a few minutes, while he took some more oxygen.

'If it's making you ill to talk, I'll go,' I said concerned.

'No it's alright,' said Albert, 'I like talking to you.'

The story of his suffering touched my heart deeply, and it made my own problems seem pretty pathetic.

When he first got cancer, he started going to the clinic at the same time as a lot of people. Now he was the sole survivor, waiting for his turn to die.

'You've lasted longer than anyone, haven't you Albert,' said his wife, as she came in the room.

It was very moving to see how devoted his wife was to him. She had nursed him continually for nine years. The poor woman looked so tired and worn out, from the strain and worry of it all. I offered to help and support them anyway I could.

'If only this pain would go,' said Albert grimacing, 'that would be something.'

'All I can do is pray for you,' I said, feeling sad.

'Would you pray now?' asked Albert's wife.

I asked Jesus to bring relief from their suffering and peace into the house. I left shortly after and promised to return in a few days. During that time I continued to pray that same prayer.

When I returned to see how Albert was, I took a christian friend with me. We sat and listened to him recall some of the lighter moments from the past. In spite of all his illnesses, he had a wonderful sense of humour.

He seemed much more at ease and cheerful than the time before.

His breathing was normal, instead of the constant wheezing and fighting for breath. The time came for us to leave, when Albert urged us to stay a bit longer.

'There is something I want to say,' he said excitedly. 'I've wanted to tell you all night, but didn't know how.'

I wondered what it could be, that was getting him so excited.

'Half an hour after you left the other night,' he said, 'something strange happened to me. All the pain left my body I was able to walk upstairs without stopping.'

It was so uplifting for me and my friend, especially after all the problems at church.

My relationship with Albert and his family deepened over the next few months. Albert was quite riddled with cancer, as various lumps appeared on his body. They weren't always painful, but he complained that they made him itch. I prayed for him daily, and asked the Lord to guide me in what I should do.

One night he showed me two new lumps, that had formed on his arm and shoulder.

'Look at these,' he said, pointing to the offending lumps, 'they're hard, like marbles.'

Before I left, I prayed for the cancer to go in the name of Jesus Christ.

Two days later, I was amazed to see that the lumps were beginning to go soft. Within another two days they had completely gone.

It was so powerful, yet very humbling to see God dissolve those cancerous lumps.

After several months Albert's health improved so much, that I didn't feel the need to go as much. However, one morning at home, I was reading the Bible from the second book of Kings. The first five verses of chapter twenty, stuck firmly in my mind. It spoke about a King who was ill and about to die. Later on in the story, a messenger went to the King and told him he would not die, but the Lord would give him life.

'I don't understand Lord, what are you trying to say to me?' I asked.

Turning through the Bible once more, it fell open at Isaiah 38, which just happened to repeat the story.

'I'm still confused Lord,' I said, 'you'll just have to lead me to the right thing.'

In the afternoon I went for a walk along the canal. To get there I had to pass the hospital entrance. As I did, a nurse who I knew came running out and called me.

'Your friend Albert, has just been rushed in by ambulance,' she said.

'He's very ill, and is close to death, so if you want to see him, you'd better hurry.'

I looked into the side ward where she said he was. It was total chaos, as several doctors were working frantically to save him. His wife and daughter were both there, and looked as though they were expecting the worst.

'His lungs have packed up,' said his wife tearfully.

'Will he be all right?' I asked, hopefully.

'I don't think so,' she said, 'I think it's all over this time.'

'He's all done in I'm afraid,' said the doctor to Albert's wife. 'His heart and lungs have just about had it, and there's really nothing more we can do for him.'

'Can't you do anything for him?' she asked, getting desperate.

'I'm sorry,' said the doctor, 'I'm afraid all we can do is to make him comfortable.'

'How long has he got?' asked Albert's wife.

'Maybe a couple of hours at the most,' he said.

While they attended to Albert, I went for a walk around the block. I was feeling pretty depressed and confused, as I thought he was better.

'Why has this happened?' I shouted, angrily at God.

I started to wonder if it was my fault for not visiting him recently. Then quite suddenly everything went quiet. It felt like something had been put over my ears to blot out all sound.

It was then I heard God speak to me directly. 'Brian, I showed you this morning that someone was going to die, now you know who it is. The words of life, you read this morning are for Albert, now go and deliver my message.'

I walked back towards the hospital, with God's word fixed clearly in my mind. On arriving back, I found Albert's wife and daughter consoling one another. For a moment it appeared I was too late, but as I got closer I was relieved to hear Albert's groaning. It was distressing to listen to him breathe, as it sounded more like someone choking. As he drifted off into semi-consciousness, he began to cry out for his dead mother. Even though he wasn't fully aware of what was happening, the fear of death was still making him struggle. After about five minutes he went quiet, as he slipped further from life. His wife invited me to take her seat by the bed.

'You can help him, can't you Brian?' she asked.

'I can't personally, but I'll pray for him,' I said trying to reassure her. As I approached the bed, the seriousness of what was happening hit me. My mind became filled with doubt, as I remembered the doctors words of gloom.

'What if I didn't hear from God,' I thought. 'If I said he wasn't going to die, and he did, that would make it worse for his family.'

Just when my fears had almost taken over, I heard the calming voice of God once more. With renewed confidence, I took my seat beside Alberts bed. I held his hand and started to gain his attention. It was difficult because he was rambling and groaning again.

'Albert, listen carefully,' I said. 'This morning God told me a man was going to die, but he also said that he would save him. That man is you Albert, understand.'

He squeezed my hand in response, as his breath was almost gone. I placed my hands gently on his chest, and prayed.

'Albert, you will not die, but live,' I prayed. 'In the name of Jesus Christ, I command this body to receive those words of life,'

As I prayed, the spirit of God began to pour out upon us both. Within a few seconds he became alert enough to begin to speak. I felt like a lightening conductor, as God's power continued to flow into Albert's body. Another few seconds went by, and then Albert started to breathe normally.

'That's it, Albert,' I said, encouraging him, 'just relax, you're going to be fine.'

Albert's wife and daughter joined me at the bedside, where we all stood and watched Albert recover.

'Brian, thank you,' said Albert's wife.

'It's not me you need to thank,' I said, 'it's Jesus, he's the one who worked the miracle.'

'I know,' she said, 'and I'll never forget him for that.'

I sat down for a while as my legs were like jelly. When I'd recovered, I left quietly, not wanting to disturb the family reunion. It took me quite a while to fully appreciate what had happened that day. God's word ministered by the Holy Spirit had brought Albert back from the brink of death. Although the world had given up on him, God hadn't. It was the most magnificent experience I'd ever had, and just confirmed that God had not forgotten me.

Several weeks later Albert was released from hospital, just in time for Christmas. I continued to visit, and encourage them to pray, and seek God for themselves. Eventually my regular visits came to an end, when Leoni began to stay with us every weekend.

Chapter Fifteen

THE FAMILY

It was a real surprise when Karen asked me to have Leoni every weekend. Although it meant quite a sacrifice for Judith, it was worth it. Leoni was nearing school age now, and I wanted to be involved as much as possible.

Everything was going well until Karen left her mother's home, and went to live with a friend. I was a bit concerned, but as her friend had two children of her own, I thought Leoni would be fine.

Sadly I was to be proved wrong, when she told me the other children were bullying her. I spoke to Karen about it, and she promised me she'd put a stop to it. Shortly after this, my worries over her safety grew when I went to collect her.

Arriving at the house, I saw Leoni sitting on the edge of the path by the road. She was doing some colouring in a book, and didn't notice the car approaching her. There wasn't any supervision as the door was locked and the curtains were drawn together. I had to almost knock the door down to get Karen's attention. I wasn't surprised when she said she didn't hear me, as the stereo was on full blast.

'What's Leoni doing outside by the road?' I said.

'I didn't know she was out there,' said Karen, startled.

'If anyone had snatched her, you wouldn't have known,' I said, trying to make a point.

'She hasn't been snatched though has she,' she snapped angrily.

It wasn't worth saying anymore, because it was obvious I wasn't getting through. All I could do was pray that things would improve.

A few weeks later, Leoni started school. I hoped that going to school would help provide her with a more secure environment. However my hopes were short-lived, when the school informed me of some problems. She was nearly always late for school, and she was being collected by different people each day.

Whenever I challenged Karen about it, she denied it, and threatened to stop my access. Everytime she threatened me, I had no choice but to back off. I had no legal rights as a father, because we were never married.

During the summer holidays Judith and I took Leoni to the coast for a couple of weeks. When we returned, Karen had moved back to her mother's house, after a row with her friend. She told me this was only a temporary arrangement until the end of the summer.

Judith and I had often discussed the possibility of Leoni living with us, but now it seemed essential.

'I'm afraid something's going to happen to her if she stays over there,' I said, to Judith.

'Let's ask Karen if she'd agree to let Leoni come to live with us,' said Judith, 'You never know, she might agree.'

'The trouble is I'm afraid she might feel threatened and shut me out altogether,' I said. We prayed about it for a few days, and finally I got the courage to ask Karen.

'How do you feel about the idea of Leoni going to school in Devizes?' I asked nervously.

'Where would she live?' she replied.

'With me and Judith I suppose,' I said, trying to avoid the question.

'I don't know, I'll have to think about it,' said Karen.

I felt relieved and a little foolish, as I drove home. It hadn't been as bad as I'd expected.

For the next few weeks we waited anxiously to receive Karen's reply, but it didn't arrive. Finally as the new school term approached I decided to ask her again.

'Have you made your mind up yet?' I asked hopefully.

'Yes, there's no way I'll ever let her come to live with you.' she replied sharply.

'You'd better make sure you keep her safe,' I said firmly, 'and get her to school everyday.'

'Of course I will,' she said.

Judith and I were both depressed at the answer, even though we half expected it. We had tried everything we could to give Leoni a secure home, but now it was out of our hands.

'If God wants her to live here, then he'll have to change Karen's mind,' I said, comforting Judith.

With only one week left until the new school term, Karen rang up unexpectedly.

'Is there a good school in Devizes, for Leoni to go to?' she said.

'I'm sorry I don't understand,' I said, feeling confused.

'I've decided to let her come and live with you,' she said, 'at least for now.'

'Yes I can sort that out, no trouble,' I said, feeling stunned.

'Right then, you'd better come and collect her then,' she said.

Within a couple of days, Leoni had moved in and was looking forward to her new school. The first thing on our agenda was to get somewhere larger to live, as we only had one bedroom. I went to see the local council about the possibility of getting a transfer.

'I'll put you on the waiting list,' said the man from the housing department. 'You never know you might get lucky, but I wouldn't expect too much if I was you.'

'I'll trust God to sort it out for me,' I said, confidently.

'Well the way the housing situation is, it'll need a miracle,' he said with a laugh.

A week later the laugh was on him when we were given a two bedroomed flat. After we'd moved in and finished decorating, we got down to the job of being a family. We soon realised that it wasn't going to be easy, as Leoni had several problems.

One of the worst things was she had a very bad diet, caused by eating too many chips and chocolate. It became quite a concern for us, because at the age of five her teeth were beginning to rot. She was also about one stone lighter than she should have been. She hadn't been used to being made to eat her vegetables, or other food she didn't like.

For many months, the dinner table became a battlefield, as we attempted to change her lifestyle. A barrier formed between Judith and I, as Leoni's eating habits came between us. We both had different ideas of how we should tackle the problem. Judith remained firm throughout the meal, but I would give way when Leoni started crying. Eventually after months of fighting we sat down and discussed it sensibly.

'We'll only succeed if we work together,' said Judith.

'I realise that,' I said. 'I know I've got to be tougher on her, but it's not easy when she cries.'

'It's not only you whose got to change,' she said. 'I could be a little softer.'

We asked God to teach us to understand Leoni and each other, and to give us all patience. Gradually the battle with Leoni began to turn in our favour, as God taught us all to work together. Just before Christmas, most of the struggle with Leoni's eating habits was over.

It was the first Christmas I'd ever spent with Leoni. To be with her when she opened her presents was a thrill I never expected to have. We took her to see Karen on Boxing day. She was now living in bed and breakfast accomodation in Salisbury. It was the first time Leoni had seen her mother in two months.

After the Christmas holidays Leoni returned to school to face her medical. She was quite worried about it because at her last school they said she was partially deaf. We talked about it, and she asked me to pray for her to be healed. Leoni was no stranger to miracles, as God had already healed her verrucas on her feet. The next day her smiling face told it's own story. She now had perfect hearing.

As Leoni's first year at school came to a close, my fears about her future returned. Karen had moved into permanent accommodation with her fiance, so I wondered if she was going take Leoni back. I had visions of all the hard work we had put into sorting Leoni out, going down the drain.

As far as the law went, I didn't have any legal rights, so I decided to talk to a solicitor. Fortunately a Christian friend of ours was a solicitor, so we were all able to pray about it.

Judith and I, both felt Leoni would have a better future with us, and be brought up to know Jesus. My problem was whether God wanted her to stay with us. Eventually after much prayer and advice I applied for a residence order. It wasn't an easy decision to make, because I didn't want to hurt Karen for Leoni's sake. I wanted Karen to hear the news from me personally, so I wrote to her explaining my decision.

A few days later she rang up and flew into a rage. 'We'll see who wins in court,' she said, 'at least I'm not the one with the criminal record.'

'I'm sorry,' I said, 'but I've only done what I think is best for Leoni.'

'My solicitor is going to take you apart,' she said, hanging up.

It was another month before we heard from Karen again, when she rang up to say she wanted Leoni to stay for three weeks. As there was only three weeks left of the summer holidays I didn't agree.

'You can have her for two weeks but not three,' I said. 'She has to be back here the final week, to get ready for school.'

'No way,' said Karen, 'you can't dictate to me.'

She started to get angry and abusive, so I hung up. An hour later she was on the phone again telling me what her solicitor had said.

'As Leoni's mother, I have all the legal rights,' she said confidently. 'I can come over and take Leoni from you anytime, and you can't stop me.'

'You can't do that,' I said, horrified.

'I can,' she said arrogantly. 'My solicitor said so, and if necessary I can bring the police.'

Suddenly the thought of the police barging in and taking Leoni away was too much for me. I didn't know what to say to her, so I prayed at her down the telephone.

'You can't keep bringing God into it,' shouted Karen's fiance back down the phone at me.

'How else am I supposed to defend myself,' I said.

'We're coming over to get her, and that's it,' he said.

'I shouldn't come, if I was you,' I said, threateningly.

Before I could say anything else I would regret, Judith snatched the phone away from me and hung up. We were so afraid of what might happen if they came up, we decided to go away for the weekend.

We contacted Judith's mother in Liverpool and left immediately. To Leoni it all seemed like a great adventure, but to us it was a nightmare. It felt like I was on the run from the police again. We notified our solicitor about what had happened, and he told us he'd sort it out.

When we returned to Devizes our solicitor had secured us an order at court, preventing Leoni being removed. For the first time ever, I had all the legal right's, although it was only temporary.

A month later the battle hotted up, as we came under attack from the opposite side. In the statements we were painted as evil religous lunatics. While Karen and her boyfriend were portrayed as kind responsible people. Even the welfare officer refused to accept that leaving a child unsupervised was wrong. Things weren't made any easier by Karen's solicitor, as it was clear she didn't like me. Whether it was because I was a Christian or something else I didn't know.

As the bizarre statements continued to arrive, I began to wonder where God was. 'What are you going to do about these lies?' I shouted angrily at God. I carried on pleading with God until a Bible verse about telling the truth came into my thoughts. 'You shall know the truth and the truth shall set you free,' it read.

Karen's position continued to improve as we got closer to the final court hearing. Finally the strain became too much for us, and we pleaded with God again. We prayed that if we lost the case, we would trust God to look after Leoni. There wasn't anything else we could do. We had to believe he was big enough to keep her safe wherever she lived.

We felt quite relieved after praying, as we realised God's will was best for everyone. Two days before the hearing we had our final briefing with our solicitor. He informed us that Karen's side had appointed a lady barrister. Her solicitor was unable to attend, because she had become too emotionally involved in it.

The night before the hearing, we held a special prayer meeting in our flat. Ten Christians came along to support us. They had been praying for us since the court proceedings first began. For two hours we read the Bible and prayed that God's will would be done. As the meeting ended, I felt prompted to pray for Karen's barrister. The only thing we knew about her was that she came from London. I prayed that either she was a Christian, or she would be sympathetic to the Christian faith.

In the morning I got up and walked the dog down the canal, and prayed once more. For a while I sat and watched the swans and their young family, and wondered if we'd still be one after lunch.

At ten o'clock we drove slowly to the court, and talked over what we should say. Our solicitor was waiting for us as we pulled into the car park near the court. He greeted us with a big beaming smile, and told us we had nothing to worry about. After thinking it was all right for him to say that, he told me why.

'You won't have to give evidence,' he said.

'Why's that?' I asked, looking puzzled.

'Karen's agreed to let Leoni stay with you,' he said happily. 'As long as you're prepared to let her have full access.'

'Yes of course,' I said, 'but what made them change their minds.'

He told us that Karen's barrister had telephoned him late last night to talk over the case. She'd been requested by Karen's solicitor to attack our Christian faith and it's way of life. She was unable to follow this line because of her own beliefs.

'Are you telling me she's a christian?' I asked.

'I think so,' he replied. 'Anyway she advised Karen to consider the offer of weekend access, and she agreed.'

The hearing only lasted a few minutes, as the agreement was drawn up officially. We were awarded a residence order and Karen received her staying access agreement.

Later after we'd all parted amicably, the reality of what God had done began to sink in.

At last my painful search for happiness was over. I had wanted to be part of a proper family all my life, now I was.

AUTHOR'S NOTE

Today my family and I attend a local church which we have found very supportive.

For the past few years I have been learning my trade as an evangelist. I share my experiences in churches, prisons and other venues, I am always looking for new opportunities.

I hope this book may have given an insight into some of the reasons why bad behaviour exists. Not that I wish to excuse myself or lay blame on any other party.

Rejection and attention seeking behaviour were the main factors which led me into crime. Thankfully meeting Jesus Christ has healed those wounds and put an end to that way of life. In conclusion we all need someone to depend on.

If like me you've never prayed before, may I suggest the prayer I prayed which can be found on page 48.

If you would like to contact me, please write to the address below:

PO Box 568, Devizes,
Wiltshire SN10 1QL.